THE YEAR Y WERE BOR

1942

A fascinating book about the year 1942 with information on:
Events of the year UK, Adverts of 1942, Cost of living, Births, Deaths, Sporting events,
Book publications, Movies, Music, World events and People in power.

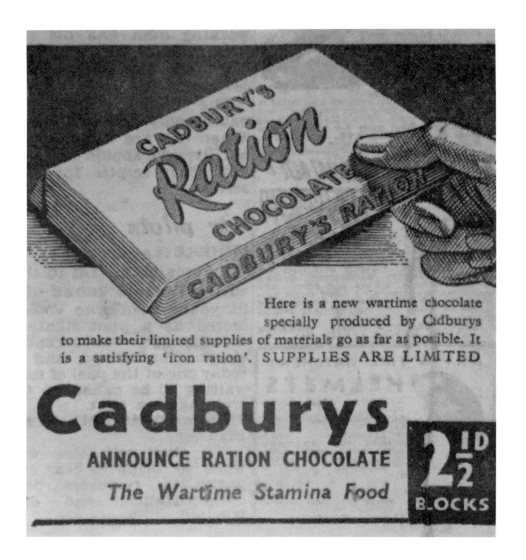

Here is a new wartime chocolate specially produced by Cadburys to make their limited supplies of materials go as far as possible. It is a satisfying 'iron ration'. SUPPLIES ARE LIMITED

Cadburys
ANNOUNCE RATION CHOCOLATE
The Wartime Stamina Food

2½D BLOCKS

INDEX

UK EVENTS OF 1942

January

1st The Sneyd Colliery Disaster was a coal mining accident on the 1st January 1942 in Burslem in the English city of Stoke-on-Trent. An underground explosion occurred at 7:50 am, caused by sparks from wagons underground igniting coal dust. A total of 57 men and boys died. Due to an old superstition that said the cutting of coal on New Year's was unlucky, miners traditionally did not work on New Year's Day; but because of the war effort, the men of Sneyd turned out to work a normal day. 295 men were working in No. 4 pit when at 7:50 am an explosion occurred in the Banbury seam which was 0.5 miles (0.80 km) underground. The force of the explosion was powerful enough to blow men off their feet; one apprentice, Reg Grocott (16) was blown around a corner and his trajectory was stopped by a water drum. The man he was working with was not so lucky having been thrown against a wall and killed.

9th The 1942 Betteshanger Miners' Strike took place from the 9th January 1942 at the Betteshanger colliery in Kent, England. The strike had its origins in a switch to a new coalface, No. 2. This face was much narrower and harder to work than the previous face and outputs were reduced. The miners proved unable to meet management production quotas and the mine owners refused to pay the previously agreed minimum daily wage, alleging deliberate slow working. An arbitrator called in to review the dispute ruled that the quotas were achievable. The miners disagreed and went on strike from 9 January. Under wartime regulations, Order 1305, striking was illegal unless the matter had been referred to the Ministry of Labour and National Service for settlement. Prosecutions were made against the strikers; three union officials were imprisoned and 1,085 men fined. The prosecutions hardened the strikers' attitudes and after the strike entered its third week the government began negotiations. A settlement was reached to reinstate the minimum wage and for the men to return to work on the 29th January. The imprisoned men received a royal pardon on the 2nd February and the fines were remitted in July 1943.

10th World War II: Liverpool Blitz ends with German bombs dropped in the Stanhope Street area of the city, with nine people dying and many more suffering injuries. Among the houses destroyed in the bombing is the former home of Adolf Hitler's half-brother Alois. Four more people die as a result of their injuries the following day. Liverpool was the most heavily bombed area of the country, outside London, due to the city having, along with Birkenhead, the largest port on the west coast and being of significant importance to the British war effort. Descriptions of damage were kept vague to hide information from the Germans, and downplayed in the newspapers for propaganda purposes; many Liverpudlians thus felt that their suffering was overlooked compared to other places. Around 4,000 people were killed in the Merseyside area during the Blitz. This death toll was second only to London, which suffered over 40,000 by the end of the war.

January

26th | World War II: First United States troops for the European theatre arrive in the UK, at Belfast.

29th | Desert Island Discs is a radio programme broadcast on BBC Radio 4. It was first broadcast on the BBC Forces Programme on the 29th January 1942. Each week a guest, called a 'castaway' during the programme, is asked to choose eight recordings (usually, but not always, music), a book and a luxury item that they would take if they were to be cast away on a desert island, whilst discussing their lives and the reasons for their choices. It was devised and originally presented by Roy Plomley. Since 2018 the programme has been presented by Lauren Laverne. More than 3,000 episodes have been recorded, with some guests having appeared more than once and some episodes featuring more than one guest. An example of a guest who falls into both categories is Bob Monkhouse, who appeared with his co-writer Denis Goodwin on 12th December 1955 and in his own right on the 20th December 1998. In February 2019 a panel of broadcasting industry experts named Desert Island Discs the "greatest radio programme of all time".

February

1st | Rationing began on the 8th January 1940 when bacon, butter and sugar were rationed. By the 1st February 1942 many other foodstuffs, including meat, milk, cheese, eggs and cooking fat were also 'on the ration'. Rationing was a means of ensuring the fair distribution of food and commodities when they were scarce. It began after the start of WW2 with petrol and later included other goods such as butter, sugar and bacon. Eventually, most foods were covered by the rationing system with the exception of fruit and vegetables. Ration books were given to everyone in Britain who then registered in a shop of their choice. When something was purchased the shopkeeper marked the purchase off in the customer's book. Special exceptions made allowing for some groups of people who required additional food like underground mine workers, members of the Women's Land Army and members of the Armed forces.

February

13th | Hitler's Operation Sealion, the invasion of England, is cancelled. By September 1940, the month in which Sea Lion was supposed to take place, the operation was postponed due in large part to the waning strength of the Luftwaffe. The Kriegsmarine suffered heavy losses in the battle for Norway a few months earlier, which also lessened the feasibility of the operation. Neither Admiral Eric Raeder, commander of the Kriegsmarine at the time, nor Hermann Göring, commander of the Luftwaffe, believed in the plan. It wasn't until 13th February 1942, however, that all units allocated for deployment in this operation were officially detached from the project and made available for other operations, marking the official end of Operation Sealion. The most notable use for those newly available troops was the ongoing combat following Operation Barbarossa.

15th | World War II: General Arthur Percival's forces surrender to the Japanese at the Battle of Singapore. The Battle of Singapore, also known as the Fall of Singapore, was fought in the South—East Asian theatre of the Pacific War when the Empire of Japan invaded the British stronghold of Singapore—nicknamed the "Gibraltar of the East". Prior to the invasion, Singapore was a major British military base and economic trading port in South—East Asia and was the key to British imperial interwar defence planning for South-East Asia and the South-West Pacific, then known as the "Far East". The fighting in Singapore lasted for about a week from the 8th to the 15th February 1942, after the two months during which Japanese forces advanced down the Malayan Peninsula.

16th | Bangka Island massacre: Japanese soldiers machine-gun 22 Australian Army nurses and 60 Australian and British soldiers and crew members from two sunken ships. Only one nurse and two soldiers survive.

19th | Clement Attlee is appointed first Deputy Prime Minister of the United Kingdom.

27th | James Stanley Hey, a British Army research officer, helps develop radio astronomy, when he discovers that the sun emits radio waves.

March

3rd | 1st combat flight for Canadian British-built Avro Lancaster bomber.

7th | 15 Mk-VB Spitfires reach Malta.

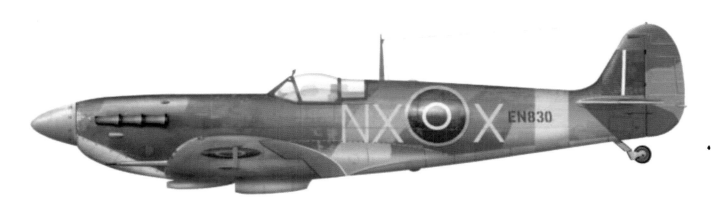

12th | British troops vacate the Andaman Islands in Gulf of Bengal.

March

28th   The St Nazaire Raid or Operation Chariot was a British amphibious attack on the heavily defended Normandie dry dock at St Nazaire in German-occupied France during the Second World War. The operation was undertaken by the Royal Navy and British Commandos under the auspices of Combined Operations Headquarters on the 28th March 1942. St Nazaire was targeted because the loss of its dry dock would force any large German warship in need of repairs, such as Tirpitz, sister ship of Bismarck, to return to home waters by running the gauntlet of the Home Fleet of the Royal Navy and other British forces, via the English Channel or the GIUK gap.

The explosive charges in HMS Campbeltown detonated at noon on 28th March 1942, and the dry dock was destroyed. Reports vary on the fate of the two tankers that were in the dock; they were either swept away by the wall of water and sunk, or swept to the far end of the dock, but not sunk. A party of 40 senior German officers and civilians who were on a tour of Campbeltown were killed. In total, the explosion killed about 360 men. The wreck of Campbeltown could still be seen inside the dry dock months later when RAF photo reconnaissance planes were sent to photograph the port.

April

1st   The Women's Timber Corps (WTC) was a British civilian organisation created on the 1st April 1942 during the Second World War to work in forestry replacing men who had left to join the armed forces. Women who joined the WTC were commonly known as Lumber Jills.

5th   World War II: Japanese Navy attacks Colombo in Ceylon (Sri Lanka). Royal Navy Cruisers HMS Cornwall and HMS Dorsetshire are sunk southwest of the island.

9th   World War II: Japanese Navy launches air raid on Trincomalee in Ceylon (Sri Lanka); Royal Navy aircraft carrier HMS Hermes and Royal Australian Navy Destroyer HMAS Vampire are sunk off the country's East Coast.

April

15th | George VI awards George Cross to people of Malta.

17th | The Augsburg Raid, also referred to as Operation Margin, was a bombing raid made by the RAF on the MAN U-boat engine plant in Augsburg undertaken during the daylight hours of the 17th April 1942. The mission was assigned to No. 44 (Rhodesia) Squadron and No. 97 Squadron, both of which were equipped with the new Avro Lancaster. The speed of the Lancaster and its large bombload capacity gave reason for optimism that the raid might succeed. It was the first of the attacks upon German industry in Augsburg.

23rd | World War II: Exeter becomes the first city bombed as part of the "Baedeker Blitz" in retaliation for the British bombing of Lübeck.

24th | Barnburgh Main Colliery. On the 24th April 1942, the mine suffered a collapse in the Park Gate coal seam. Miners reported that the floor rose up towards the ceiling. Geologists put forward the theory that the downward pressure caused the floor to be forced upwards. 18 miners were sealed in and despite frantic rescue efforts, four men died. The last two bodies were located and removed from the pit on the 30th April 1942 some six days after the disaster.

25th | Over the weekend of 25th – 27th April 1942, Bath suffered three raids, from 80 Luftwaffe aircraft which took off from Nazi occupied northern France. As the city sirens wailed, few citizens took cover, even when the first pathfinder flares fell. The people of Bath still believed the attack was destined for nearby Bristol. During the previous four months, Bristol had been hit almost every night, so the people of Bath did not expect the bombs to fall on them. The first raid struck just before 11 pm on the Saturday night and lasted until 1 am. The German aircraft then returned to France, refuelled, rearmed and returned at 4.35 am. Bath was still on fire from the first raid, making it easier for the German bombers to pick out their targets. The third raid, which only lasted two hours but caused extensive damage, commenced in the early hours of Monday morning. The bombers flew low to drop their high explosives and incendiaries, and then returned to rake the streets with machine-gun fire.

May

5th | Battle of Madagascar; British commander Robert Sturges leads the invasion of Vichy French-held Madagascar.

6th | The Radio Doctor (Charles Hill) makes his first BBC radio broadcast giving avuncular health care advice.

15th | RMS Queen Mary arrives at Greenock with nearly 10,000 U.S. troops aboard.

19th | A subsequently famous BBC outside broadcast recording captures the song of the common nightingale with the sound of Royal Air Force Lancaster bombers flying overhead.

25th | A breach in the Glamorganshire Canal near Nantgarw is inspected but it is decided not to do any work on it; the canal closes permanently later in the year.

30th | World War II: First RAF "thousand bomber raid" sets off to carry out the bombing of Cologne in Germany. The German city of Cologne was bombed in 262 separate air raids by the Allies during World War II, all by the Royal Air Force (RAF) but for a single failed post-capture test of a guided missile by the United States Army Air Forces. A total of 34,711 long tons of bombs were dropped on the city by the RAF. 20,000 people died during the war in Cologne due to aerial bombardments.

June

5th British offensive in North Africa under General Ritchie. North Africa and the Middle East — The Eighth Army, fighting in the North African Campaign, was the only British land force engaging the German Army anywhere in the world. After some early successes against the Italians the British were pushed back following the arrival of the Afrika Korps under Erwin Rommel.

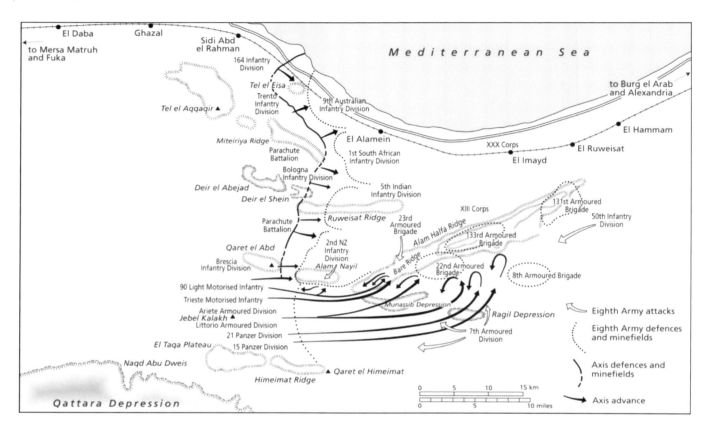

6th First Human Test of a Nylon Parachute –On the 6th June 1942, Adeline Gray made the first jump by a human with a nylon parachute at Brainard Field in Hartford. Her jump, performed before a group of Army officials, put the world's first nylon parachute to the test.

11th The First Battle of El Alamein was a battle of the Western Desert Campaign of the Second World War, fought in Egypt between Axis forces (Germany and Italy) of the Panzer Army Africa (which included the Afrika Korps under Field Marshal Erwin Rommel) and Allied (British Imperial and Commonwealth) forces of the Eighth Army. The British prevented a second advance by the Axis forces into Egypt. Axis positions near El Alamein, only 66 mi (106 km) from Alexandria, were dangerously close to the ports and cities of Egypt, the base facilities of the Commonwealth forces and the Suez Canal. However, the Axis forces were too far from their base at Tripoli in Libya to remain at El Alamein indefinitely, which led both sides to accumulate supplies for more offensives, against the constraints of time and distance.

15th Next of Kin was released. Next of Kin is a 1942 Second World War propaganda film produced by Ealing Studios. The film was originally commissioned by the British War Office as a training film to promote the government message that "Careless talk costs lives". After being taken on by Ealing Studios, the project was expanded and given a successful commercial release. After the war and up until at least the mid-1960s, services in British Commonwealth countries continued to use The Next of Kin as part of security training. The film's title is derived from the phrase "the next of kin have been informed" as used by radio announcers when reporting on the loss of personnel in action.

June

21st | US President Franklin D. Roosevelt and British Prime Minister Winston Churchill arrive in Washington, D.C.

23rd | World War II: Germany's latest fighter, a Focke-Wulf FW190 is captured intact when it mistakenly lands at RAF Pembrey in Wales.

25th | Using every available aircraft in RAF Bomber Command and some of other commands, a thousand-bomber raid was mounted against Bremen. 1,067 aircraft (472 Wellingtons, 124 Halifaxes, 96 Lancasters, 69 Stirlings, 51 Blenheims, 50 Handley Page Hampdens, 50 Whitleys, 24 Douglas Bostons, 20 Manchesters and de Havilland Mosquitos), 102 Lockheed Hudsons and Wellingtons of RAF Coastal Command, and 5 RAF Army Cooperation Command. Those of No. 5 Group RAF - 142 aircraft – bombed the Focke-Wulf factory; 20 Blenheims were allocated to the AG Weser shipyard; the RAF Coastal Command aircraft were to bomb the DeSchiMAG shipyard; all other aircraft were to carry out an area attack on the "town and docks". The limited success was entirely due to the use of GEE, which enabled the leading crews to start marker fires through the cloud cover. 696 Bomber Command aircraft were able to claim attacks on Bremen. 572 houses were completely destroyed and 6,108 damaged. 85 people were killed, 497 injured and 2,378 bombed out. At the Focke-Wulf factory, an assembly shop was completely flattened, 6 buildings were seriously damaged and 11 buildings lightly so. The Atlas Werke, the Bremer Vulkan shipyard, the Norddeutsche Hütte, the Korff refinery, and two large dockside warehouses were also damaged. 48 Bomber Command aircraft were lost (a new record 5% of those dispatched), including 4 which came down in the sea near England from which all but 2 crew members were rescued. This time, the heaviest casualties were suffered by the OTUs of No. 91 Group RAF, which lost 23 of the 198 Whitleys and Wellingtons provided by that group, a loss of 11.6 per cent. 5 of the 102 Coastal Command aircraft were also lost.

British premier Winston Churchill travels from US to London.

30th | U-boats sink and damage 146 allied ships this month (700,227 tons).

July

1st | Military scientists begin testing of anthrax as a biological warfare agent on Gruinard Island.

2nd | J. Arthur Rank's Odeon Cinemas purchase UK sites of Paramount Cinemas.

7th | John Maynard Keynes takes his seat in the British House of Lords as Baron Keynes of Tilton after being knighted.

10th | the patriotic Academy Award-winning drama film Mrs. Miniver, starring Greer Garson, is released in London.

11th | RAF Lancaster bombers flew the longest raid of the European theatre up to this time, traveling 1,750 miles to bomb German shipyards at Danzig.

17th | Winston Churchill informed Stalin that, in light of the PQ 17 disaster, no further convoys would be sent to northern Russia in the foreseeable future.

26th | During the First Battle of El Alamein, British troops launched Operation Manhood in a final attempt to break the Axis forces. 403 British bombers raided Hamburg, killing 337 and rendering 14,000 homeless. 14 bombers were lost.

July

28th Arthur Harris made a radio broadcast informing German listeners that the bombers would soon be coming "every night and every day, rain, blow or snow - we and the Americans. I have just spent eight months in America, so I know exactly what is coming. We are going to scourge the Third Reich from end to end, if you make it necessary for us to do so ... it is up to you to end the war and the bombing. You can overthrow the Nazis and make peace."

31st 630 British bombers raided Düsseldorf, destroying 453 buildings and killing 276 civilians. 29 bombers were lost.

Driving for pleasure was banned in Britain because of fuel shortage.

August

3rd The British launched Operation Pedestal, an effort to get desperately needed supplies to Malta.

5th Anthony Eden announced in the House of Commons that the Munich Agreement of 1938 would play no part in the post-war settlement of Czechoslovakia's borders, because the British government no longer considered itself bound to that agreement since the Germans destroyed it.

6th The British submarine HMS Thorn went missing off southern Crete, probably sunk by the Italian torpedo boat Pegaso.

7th Winston Churchill visited the British troops at El Alamein.

9th The Walt Disney animated film Bambi had its world premiere in London.

August

11th The British aircraft carrier HMS Eagle was torpedoed and sunk by the German submarine U-73 during Operation Pedestal.

13th During Operation Pedestal the British cruiser Manchester was torpedoed and heavily damaged by two Italian motor torpedo boats and then scuttled.

14th British Commandos carried out Operation Barricade, an overnight raid on an anti-aircraft gun and radar site northwest of Pointe de Saire, France.

19th The Dieppe Raid took place on the northern coast of France. The operation was virtually a complete failure and almost 60% of the 6,086 men who made it ashore were killed, wounded or captured. The British destroyer Berkeley was crippled by Focke-Wulf Fw 190s and scuttled.

26th The British government lifted the ban on the communist newspaper The Daily Worker.

29th British destroyer Eridge was permanently disabled off El Daba, Egypt by an Italian torpedo boat.

September

2nd British Commandos conducted Operation Dryad, an overnight raid on the Casquets lighthouse in the Channel Islands.

3rd The Brains Trust first broadcast under this title on BBC Home Service radio.

7th Operation Branford was a British Commando raid during the Second World War. The target of the raid was the island of Burhou in the Channel Islands. The raiding force was supplied by No. 62 Commando also known as the Small-Scale Raiding Force was commanded by Captain Ogden-Smith and consisted of 11 men. The raid took place a few days after the successful Operation Dryad over the night of 7/8 September 1942. Their objective was to establish whether the island was suitable as an artillery battery position to support an attack on Alderney.

8th Winston Churchill reviewed the course of the war in an address to the British House of Commons.

10th The RAF dropped 100,000 bombs on Düsseldorf in less than an hour.

12th The British troopship RMS Laconia was torpedoed and sunk off the coast of West Africa by the German submarine U-156. U-boats were then dispatched to the area to pick up survivors.

15th British submarine Talisman went missing in the Mediterranean, possibly lost to a naval mine off Sicily.

17th The British war film In Which We Serve, directed by Noël Coward and David Lean, was released in the United Kingdom.

23rd The British Council of Churches, an ecumenical organisation, is established, as is the Council of Christians and Jews.

British forces occupied Antananarivo in Madagascar.

September

25th   Four British de Havilland Mosquito bombers conducted the Oslo Mosquito raid, intended to boost morale of the Norwegian people. The operation failed as the Mosquito bombs failed to destroy the Gestapo HQ but caused 80 civilian casualties and one bomber was lost.

26th   The British destroyer Veteran was torpedoed and sunk in the Atlantic Ocean by German submarine U-404.

29th   Operation Braganza was launched on the night of the 29th September 1942 by Lieutenant General Brian Horrocks, commanding British XIII Corps. It was intended as a preliminary to Operation Lightfoot, part of the Second Battle of El Alamein. The objective was to capture an area of ground near Deir el Munassib in Egypt, to be used for extra artillery deployment. This would involve the 131st (Queen's) Infantry Brigade from the 44th (Home Counties) Division, supporting armour from the 4th Armoured Brigade, nine field regiments and one medium battery of artillery.

October

1st   The British Army formed the new unit, Royal Electrical and Mechanical Engineer. (REME).

2nd   The British light cruiser Curacoa sank north of Ireland after an accidental collision with the troop transport Queen Mary. It was one of the Royal Navy's worst accidental losses of the war.

3rd   On the night of 3–4 October 1942 twelve men from the Special Operations Executive Commanded No. 62 Commando (also known as the "Small Scale Raiding Force") and No. 12 Commando, left Portland on MTB 344 at 1900 and landed on Sark with the object of offensive reconnaissance and capturing prisoners.

5th   Oxford Committee for Famine Relief founded. Oxfam is a confederation of 20 independent charitable organizations focusing on the alleviation of global poverty, founded in 1942 and led by Oxfam International. It is a major non-profit group with an extensive collection of operations.

8th   A Nazi radio announcement stated that officers and men captured in the Dieppe raid had been manacled in retaliation for the alleged tying of prisoners during the Sark raid. The British War Office replied that German prisoners of war captured at Dieppe had not had their hands tied and if the Germans did not immediately unshackle their prisoners, then German POWs in Canada would be put in chains starting on the 10th October.

October

10th	The British troopship Orcades was torpedoed and sunk near Cape Town by German submarine U-172. 1,022 were rescued but 45 perished.
14th	German auxiliary cruiser Komet was torpedoed and sunk in the English Channel by a British motor torpedo boat.
15th	German submarine U-661 was sunk in the North Atlantic by depth charges from the British destroyer Viscount. HMS Viscount was a V-class destroyer (Thornycroft V and W class) of the British Royal Navy that saw service in the final months of World War I and in World War II.
17th	British cargo ship Empire Chaucer was torpedoed and sunk off Cape Town, South Africa by German submarine U-504.
23rd	The Royal Air Force conducted its heaviest raid on Genoa to date.
26th	The Defence of Outpost Snipe in Egypt, took place in the Second Battle of El Alamein, part of the Western Desert campaign during the Second World War. On the night of 26th /27th October 1942, the 2nd Battalion of the Rifle Brigade (part of the 7th Motor Brigade), with thirteen 6-pounder anti-tank guns and the 239th Battery, 76th (Royal Welch Fusiliers) Anti-Tank Regiment, Royal Artillery, with six more 6-pounders, was ordered to occupy a desert feature known as Snipe, a small depression in the landscape 1.5 mi (2.4 km) south-west of Kidney Ridge that was suitable for an outpost. Once consolidated, it could be used as a jumping-off point for an advance by the 24th Armoured Brigade.
28th	On the second anniversary of Ohi Day, Winston Churchill made a speech to the Greek people telling them that their "courage and spirit in adversity remain a lively inspiration to the United Nations. Outside their own country the armed forces of Greece, the navy, army and air force, are once again in the field already testing their growing strength in the face of the enemy, and anxious for the day, not far off now, when they will be with you and avenging your sufferings."
29th	Leading British clergymen and political figures held a public meeting to express their outrage at the persecution of Jews by Nazi Germany. Churchill sent a message to the meeting stating that "Free men and women denounce these vile crimes, and when this world struggle ends with the enthronement of human rights, racial persecution will be ended."
31st	30 planes of the Luftwaffe bombed Canterbury in one of the heaviest raids on England since the Blitz.

November

2nd	The BBC began French-language broadcasts to Canada.
4th	Second Battle of El Alamein effectively ends with Erwin Rommel forced to order German forces to retreat this evening in the face of pressure from General Montgomery's Eighth Army. Clearing up operations continue until the 11th November.
6th	The Church of England abolished its rule requiring women to wear hats in church.
8th	British and American forces began Operation Torch, the invasion of French North Africa.

November

10th | Winston Churchill took to the podium at the Lord Mayor's Luncheon in London with news of the Allied victory at El Alamein. "Now this is not the end," Churchill said. "It is not even the beginning of the end. But it is, perhaps, the end of the beginning."

11th | British Commandos conducted Operation Fahrenheit, an overnight raid on a signals station at Point de Plouézec, France.

13th | Montgomery captured Tobruk, squeezing Rommel between two large advancing Allied forces.

Bernard Law Montgomery   **Erwin Rommel**

19th | Operation Freshman: A British airborne force landed using gliders in Norway with the intent of sabotaging a chemical plant in Telemark that the Germans could use for their atomic weapons programme. Neither of the two aircraft-glider forces were able to land near their objective and the operation ended in failure with 41 killed.

20th | The British Eighth Army retook Benghazi.

25th | The British Special Operations Executive (SOE) in co-operation with Greek Resistance fighters executed Operation Harling, destroying the heavily guarded Gorgopotamos viaduct.

28th | The British troopship Nova Scotia was torpedoed and sunk in the Indian Ocean by German submarine U-177 with the loss of 858 out of 1,052 people aboard.

29th | The British destroyer Ithuriel was bombed and damaged beyond repair at Bône, Algeria by the Luftwaffe.

December

1st   The Beveridge Report, officially entitled Social Insurance and Allied Services (Cmd. 6404), is a government report, published, influential in the founding of the welfare state in the United Kingdom. It was drafted by the Liberal economist William Beveridge, who proposed widespread reforms to the system of social welfare to address what he identified as "five giants on the road of reconstruction": "Want... Disease, Ignorance, Squalor and Idleness". Published in the midst of World War II, the report promised rewards for everyone's sacrifices. Overwhelmingly popular with the public, it formed the basis for the post-war reforms known as the Welfare State, which include the expansion of National Insurance and the creation of the National Health Service.

6th   93 aircraft of the Royal Air Force conducted a daylight bombing raid on Eindhoven targeting the Philips Radio Works. The building was heavily damaged but the RAF lost 13 planes in the attack.

7th   The British ocean liner Ceramic was torpedoed and sunk west of the Azores by German submarine U-515. There was only one survivor of the 657 people aboard and he was taken aboard U-515 as a prisoner of war.

10th   British and Canadian governments announced that they had given instructions that German prisoners of war were to be unshackled on the 12th December.

12th   The Royal Navy submarine P222 was most likely sunk off Capri by an Italian torpedo boat.

13th   Jews in Britain observed a day of mourning for the victims of Nazi genocide.

17th   While escorting the convoy ON 153, the British destroyer Firedrake was torpedoed and sunk by German submarine U-211.

18th   The British P-class destroyer Partridge was torpedoed and sunk west of Oran by German submarine U-565.

21st   British troops crossed from India back into Burma and headed toward Akyab.

25th   British submarine P48 was sunk in the Gulf of Tunis by Italian torpedo boats.

30th   British insurance companies attack the Beveridge Report.

31st   Maunsell Forts erected in the Thames Estuary.

APPLEBY BOILER PLATES

Practical experience over a long period has proved that Appleby Basic Boiler Plates are highly satisfactory in manipulation and in service under the stringent conditions met in locomotive boilers and fireboxes. Equally suitable for welding or riveting.

The illustrations were taken at the G.W.R Boiler Shops, Swindon, by courtesy of the Chief Mechanical Engineer.

WELD OR RIVET

JOINT USING WELD CAULKING

FIREBOX MADE WITH APPLEBY BOILER PLATES

* DUCTILITY..
* FLATNESS...
* ACCURACY OF THICKNESS & SHEARING..
* GOOD FINISH.

THE UNITED STEEL COMPANIES LTD

APPLEBY-FRODINGHAM STEEL CO. LTD.

SCUNTHORPE   Associated with The United Steel Companies Limited   LINCOLNSHIRE

AF 89

JOSEPH STAINTON *presents*

LOVE, HONOR... AND "CRISPER" TOAST!

Here's a husband whose toast will be the way he wants it ... whether crisp and crunchy — like mother used to make in the oven — or soft and hot with a golden brown shell. Proctor, the pop-up toaster with the *Crisper*, makes delicious toast for each individual taste. Just right — exactly as brown; exactly as crisp; because it's toasted inside and outside. The *Crisper* does it. So ... keep it toasting.

PROCTOR
DUAL-AUTOMATIC
The *Pop-Up* TOASTER with the CRISPER

"THIS MAKES IT DIFFERENT"

CAUTION: DON'T DUNK

Never, never put toaster in water. To keep it gleaming, wipe carefully with a damp (not wet) cloth.

TO UNPLUG— DON'T TUG

Long distance unplugging ruins electric appliance cords. To remove, grasp *plug*, pull gently.

SERVICE ASSURED

Proctor service stations are on the job — coast to coast — to provide service and genuine repair parts.

How to locate nearest Proctor Authorized Service Station

1. Consult "classified pages" in your telephone book under "Electrical Appliances."
2. See instruction booklet.
3. See any Proctor dealer.

Proctor repair parts and service are — *and will continue to be* — readily available. Proctor Electric Co., Sales Div., Proctor & Schwartz, Inc., Phila. Est. 1883

COST OF LIVING 1942

A conversion of pre-decimal to decimal money

The Pound, 1971 became the year of decimalization when the pound became 100 new pennies. Prior to that the pound was equivalent to 20 shillings. Money prior to 1971 was written £/s/d. (d being for pence). Below is a chart explaining the monetary value of each coin before and after 1971.

Symbol	Before 1971	After 1971
£	Pound (240 pennies)	Pound (100 new pennies)
s	Shilling (12 pennies)	5 pence
d	Penny	¼ of a penny
¼d	Farthing	1 penny
½d	Halfpenny	½ pence
3d	Threepence	About 1/80 of a pound
4d	Groat (four pennies)	
6d	Sixpence (Tanner)	2½ new pence
2s	Florin (2 shillings)	10 pence
2s/6d	Half a crown (2 shillings and 6 pence)	12½ pence
5s	Crown	25 pence
10s	10 shilling note (10 bob)	50 pence
10s/6d	½ Guinea	52½ pence
21s	1 Guinea	105 pence

Prices are in equivalent to new pence and inflation today and on average throughout the UK.

Item	1942	Price in today's money
Wages, average yearly	£201.00	£9,138.00
Average house price	£575.00	£26,163.00
Price of an average car	£315.00	£14,333.00
Litre of petrol	£0.02p	£1.06p
Flour 1.5kg	£0.03p	£1.41p
Bread (loaf)	£0.01p	£0.68p
Sugar 1kg	£0.03p	£1.27p
Milk 1 pint	£0.07p	£3.28p
Butter 250g	£0.04p	£2.00p
Cheese 400g	£0.05p	£2.17p
Potatoes 2.5kg	£0.03p	£1.14p
Bacon 400g	£0.14p	£6.26p
Beer (Pint)	£0.05p	£3.85p

How much did things cost in 1942?

Embassy cigarettes	**10 for 10d (5p)**
Wisdom toothbrushes	**2/5 (12p) each**
Eve toilet soap	**3d (1½p) per bar**
Palmolive toilet soap	**4d (2p) per bar**

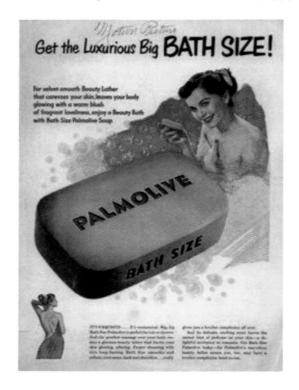

Vim	**6d (2½p) per canister**
Hartley's headlamp masks	**10/6 (52½p) to 12/6 (62½p) each**

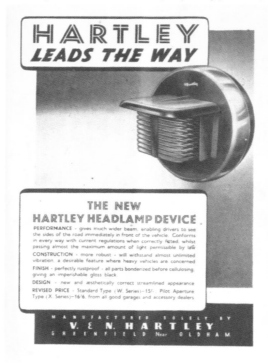

Rationing began on 8th January 1940 when bacon, butter and sugar were rationed. By 1942 many other foodstuffs, including meat, milk, cheese, eggs and cooking fat were also 'on the ration'.

This is a typical weekly food ration for an adult:

Bacon & Ham	4 oz
Other meat	value of 1 shilling and 2 pence (equivalent to 2 chops)
Butter	2 oz
Cheese	2 oz
Margarine	4 oz
Cooking fat	4 oz
Milk	3 pints
Sugar	8 oz
Preserves	1 lb every 2 months
Tea	2 oz
Eggs	1 fresh egg (plus allowance of dried egg)

Sweets	12 oz every 4 weeks
Cadbury's Ration Chocolate	2½d (1p) per bar, the supply was very limited

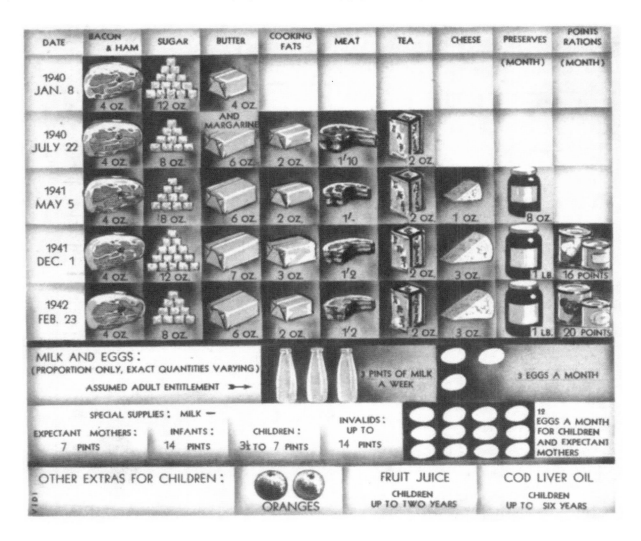

BRITISH BIRTHS

John Edward Thaw, CBE was born on the 3rd January 1942 and sadly passed away on the 21st February 2002. He was an English actor who appeared in a range of television, stage, and cinema roles. John Thaw will perhaps be best remembered for two roles: the hard-bitten, tough-talking Flying Squad detective Jack Regan in the Thames Television/ITV series The Sweeney (1975–1978), which established him as a major star in the United Kingdom. The series had two film spin-offs. Thaw was only 32 when he was cast in The Sweeney, although many viewers thought he was older. The second role was the quietly spoken, introspective, well-educated and bitter detective. Detective Chief Inspector Endeavour Morse in Inspector Morse (1987–93). A heavy drinker until going teetotal in 1995, and a heavy smoker from the age of 12, Thaw was diagnosed with cancer of the oesophagus in June 2001. Just before Christmas 2001 he was informed that the cancer had spread and the prognosis was terminal. He died on 21st February 2002, seven weeks after his 60th birthday.

Jan Leeming was born Janet Dorothy Atkins on the 5th January 1942 and is an English TV presenter and newsreader. She worked as an actress and presenter in Australia and New Zealand before becoming a well-known face on British television in regional and children's programmes. She has kept a relatively low profile since leaving the newsroom in 1987, with bit parts and one-off specials including as a stand-in newsreader for the Channel 4's breakfast show The Big Breakfast during the 1990s. Since 2000, much of her time has been spent in corporate work and her long-time passion working with a cheetah conservation charity in South Africa. She appeared in Safari School, a reality television series, which was first broadcast on BBC Two during January and February 2007. In November 2006, Leeming was a contestant on the sixth series of I'm a Celebrity...Get Me Out of Here! on ITV. Jan Leeming has done a record number of six 'Bush Tucker' trials. For one of the trials, Leeming volunteered and for the other five she was voted to do them by the British public.

Stephen William Hawking CH CBE FRS FRSA was born on the 8th January 1942 and died on the 14th March 2018. He was an English theoretical physicist, cosmologist, and author. Stephen Hawking was born in Oxford into a family of doctors. Hawking began his university education at University College, Oxford in October 1959 at the age of 17, where he received a first-class BA (Hons.) degree in physics. He began his graduate work at Trinity Hall, Cambridge in October 1962, where he obtained his PhD degree in applied mathematics and theoretical physics, specialising in general relativity and cosmology in March 1966. During this period—in 1963—Stephen was diagnosed with an early-onset slow-progressing form of motor neurone disease. Hawking's scientific works included a collaboration with Roger Penrose on gravitational singularity theorems in the framework of general relativity and the theoretical prediction that black holes emit radiation, often called Hawking radiation. He died at the age of 76, after living with motor neurone disease for more than 50 years.

Michael Patrick Smith, CBE was born on the 19th January 1942, known professionally as Michael Crawford and is an English actor, comedian and singer. At age nineteen, he was approached to play an American, Junior Sailen, in the film The War Lover (1962), which starred Steve McQueen. Michael Crawford's acting career took off again after he appeared on the London stage in the farce No Sex Please, We're British, in which he played the part of frantic chief cashier Brian Runnicles. Crawford was not the first choice for the role of Frank Spencer in Some Mothers Do 'Ave 'Em. Originally, the part had been offered to comedy actor Ronnie Barker but after he and Norman Wisdom had turned it down, Crawford took on the challenge, adopting a similar characterisation to that which he used when playing Brian Runnicles. Cast alongside him was actress Michele Dotrice in the role of Frank's long-suffering wife, Betty, and the series premiered in 1973. In 2002, in the television poll 100 Greatest Britons, he was voted the Greatest living Briton, and the seventeenth overall.

Terence Graham Parry Jones was born on the 1st February 1942 and sadly passed away on the 21st January 2020. He was a Welsh actor, writer, comedian, screenwriter, film director, historian, and member of the Monty Python comedy team. Jones wrote many books and screenplays, including comic works and more serious writing on medieval history. A member of the Campaign for Real Ale, Jones also had interest in real ale and in 1977 co-founded the Penrhos Brewery, a microbrewery at Penrhos Court at Penrhos, Herefordshire, which ran until 1983. In October 2006, Jones was diagnosed with colon cancer and underwent surgery. After a complete cycle of chemotherapy, he became free of cancer. In 2015, Jones was diagnosed with primary progressive aphasia, a form of frontotemporal dementia that impairs the ability to speak and communicate. He had first given cause for concern during the Monty Python reunion show Monty Python Live (Mostly) in July 2014 because of difficulties learning his lines. Jones died from complications of dementia on the 21st January 2020.

Alan Leonard Hunt was born on the 7th February 1942 and passed away on the 14th March 2007. He was known as Gareth Hunt and was a British actor best remembered for playing footman Frederick Norton in Upstairs, Downstairs and Mike Gambit in The New Avengers. Hunt began his television career in 1968, playing Private Kitson in one episode of the UK series Frontier. In 1976, the year after leaving Upstairs, Downstairs, Hunt starred alongside Joanna Lumley and Patrick Macnee in The New Avengers. The show's producers said Hunt was cast because of his part in Upstairs, Downstairs. He played secret agent Mike Gambit and starred in the show until its end after two series in 1977. Hunt starred in a series of television adverts for the instant coffee brand Nescafé in the 1980s, with a trademark move: to shake his closed hand then open it, to reveal coffee beans, and smell the aroma. Hunt died of pancreatic cancer, from which he had suffered for two years, on the 14th March 2007 at the age of 65, at his home in Redhill, Surrey. He was married three times and had a son by each marriage.

Lewis Brian Hopkin Jones was born on the 28th February 1942 and died on the 3rd July 1969. He was an English musician and composer, best known as the founder and original leader of the Rolling Stones. After he founded the Rolling Stones as a British blues outfit in 1962, and gave the band its name, Jones' fellow band members Keith Richards and Mick Jagger began to take over the band's musical direction. When Jones developed alcohol and drug problems, his performance in the studio became increasingly unreliable, leading to a diminished role within the band he had founded.

In June 1969, the Rolling Stones dismissed Jones; guitarist Mick Taylor took his place in the group. Jones died less than a month later, drowning in the swimming pool at his home at the age of 27. Jones' death was referenced in songs by many other pop-bands, and was the subject of poems by Pete Townshend and Jim Morrison. Referring to Jones, the Rolling Stones' Bill Wyman lamented the waste of a great innovator. In 1989, the Rolling Stones, including Jones, were inducted into the Rock and Roll Hall of Fame.

Michael York, OBE. He was born Michael Hugh Johnson on the 27th March 1942 and is an English actor. York starred as D'Artagnan in the 1973 adaptation of The Three Musketeers and he made his Broadway début in the original production of Tennessee Williams's Out Cry. One year later the sequel to The Three Musketeers was released (roughly covering events in the second half of the book) titled The Four Musketeers. Fifteen years later, most of the cast (and crew) joined together in a third film titled The Return of the Musketeers based on the Dumas novel Twenty Years After.

He played the title character in the film adaptation of Logan's Run (1976), a fugitive who tries to escape a computer-controlled society. The following year, he starred in The Island of Dr. Moreau opposite Burt Lancaster. In 2013, York announced he was suffering from the rare disease called amyloidosis. Doctors initially thought he had bone cancer. In 2012, he underwent a stem cell transplant, which can alleviate symptoms.

Neil Gordon Kinnock, **Baron Kinnock, PC** was born on the 28th March 1942 and is a British politician. As a member of the Labour Party, he served as a Member of Parliament from 1970 until 1995, first for Bedwellty and then for Islwyn. Born and raised in South Wales, Kinnock was first elected to the House of Commons in the 1970 general election. He became the Labour Party's shadow education minister after the Conservatives won power in the 1979 general election. After the party under Michael Foot suffered a landslide defeat to Margaret Thatcher in the 1983 election, Kinnock was elected Leader of the Labour Party and Leader of the Opposition. He went on to become the Vice-President of the European Commission under Romano Prodi from 1999–2004, before being elevated to the House of Lords as Baron Kinnock in 2005. Kinnock strongly opposed Brexit. In 2018, Kinnock stated, "The truth is that we can either take the increasingly plain risks and costs of leaving the EU or have the stability, growth and revenues vital for crucial public services like the NHS and social care. Recognising that, we should stop Brexit to save the NHS – or, at very least, mitigate the damage by seeking European Economic Area membership."

Norman Stewart Hughson Lamont, Baron Lamont of Lerwick, PC. He was born on the 8th May 1942 and is a British politician and former Conservative MP for Kingston-upon-Thames. Before entering parliament, he worked for N M Rothschild & Sons, the investment bank, and became director of Rothschild Asset Management. Lamont stood as a candidate for Member of Parliament in the June 1970 general election for Kingston upon Hull East. He was defeated by John Prescott, who went on to become Tony Blair's Deputy Prime Minister.

Two years later, on the 4th May 1972, Lamont won a by-election to become MP for Kingston-upon-Thames. In 1998 the former military dictator of Chile, General Augusto Pinochet visited Britain to obtain medical treatment. This prompted a debate about whether he should be arrested and put on trial over his human rights record. Lamont joined with Margaret Thatcher in defending Pinochet, calling him a "good and brave and honourable soldier". His stance was highly controversial.

Norbert Peter Stiles MBE was born on the 18th May 1942 and sadly passed away on the 30th October 2020. He was an English footballer and manager. He played for England for five years, winning 28 caps and scoring one goal. He played every minute of England's victorious 1966 FIFA World Cup campaign. In the semi-final of that tournament against Portugal, he was given the job of marking the prolific Eusébio. His tough performance resulted in Eusébio being practically nullified for the entire game. Stiles also played in the final, which England won 4–2 against West Germany. His post-match dance on the Wembley pitch, holding the World Cup trophy in one hand and his false teeth in the other, was widely broadcast. Stiles spent the majority of his club career for Manchester United, spending eleven years at Old Trafford, where he became renowned for his tough tackling and ball-winning qualities. With the Red Devils, he won two League titles and one European Cup. Stiles is one of only three Englishmen, alongside Bobby Charlton and Ian Callaghan, to have won both the World Cup and European Cup.

Doug Mountjoy was born on the 8th June 1942 and died on the 14th February 2021. He was a Welsh snooker player from Tir-y-Berth, Gelligaer, Glamorgan, Wales. Mountjoy's first professional tournament, which he entered as a late replacement, was the 1977 Masters at the New London Theatre. After defeating former world champions John Pulman, Fred Davis, and Alex Higgins to reach the final, he beat the defending Masters champion and reigning world champion Ray Reardon 7–6 to win the title. At the 1977 World Championship a couple of months later, he defeated Higgins again in the first round but lost to Dennis Taylor in the quarter-final 11–13. After being part of the winning Wales team in the first two snooker World Challenge Cups, in 1979 and 1980, he had an attack of Bell's palsy which partially paralysed his face. Mountjoy died on 14th February 2021, at the age of 78 after a stroke. In a joint statement, World Snooker chairman Barry Hearn and World Professional Billiards and Snooker Association chairman Jason Ferguson said: "Doug was first and foremost a lovely man, who had great friendships with many players".

Sir James Paul McCartney CH MBE was born on the 18th June 1942. He is an English singer, songwriter, musician, and record and film producer who gained worldwide fame as co-lead vocalist and bassist for the Beatles. A self-taught musician, McCartney is proficient on bass, guitar, keyboards, and drums. At the age of fifteen on the 6th July 1957, McCartney met John Lennon and his band, the Quarrymen, at the St Peter's Church Hall fête in Woolton. The Quarrymen played a mix of rock and roll and skiffle. Soon afterwards, the members of the band invited McCartney to join as a rhythm guitarist, and he formed a close working relationship with Lennon. Harrison joined in 1958 as lead guitarist, followed by Lennon's art school friend Stuart Sutcliffe on bass, in 1960. By May 1960, the band had tried several names, including Johnny and the Moondogs, Beatals and the Silver Beetles. They adopted the name the Beatles in August 1960 and recruited drummer Pete Best. In 1970, McCartney continued his musical career with his first solo release, McCartney, a US number-one album.

Michael John Kells Fleetwood was born on the 24th June 1947 and is a British musician and actor, best known as the drummer, co-founder, and leader of the rock band Fleetwood Mac. Born in Redruth, Cornwall, Fleetwood lived in Egypt and Norway for much of his childhood years as his father travelled with the Royal Air Force. Choosing to follow his musical interests, Fleetwood travelled to London at the age of 15, eventually combining with Peter Green, Jeremy Spencer and Bob Brunning, at Green's behest, to become the first incarnation of Fleetwood Mac. Fleetwood would remain the only member to stay with the band through its ever-changing line-up. After several album releases and line-up changes, the group moved to the United States in 1974 in an attempt to boost the band's success. Here Fleetwood invited Lindsey Buckingham and Stevie Nicks to join. Buckingham and Nicks contributed to much of Fleetwood Mac's later commercial success, including the celebrated album Rumours.

Desmond Michael Lynam, OBE was born on the 17th September 1942 and is an Irish-born television and radio presenter. Lynam started his career in broadcasting as a freelance radio journalist on BBC Radio Brighton (1968–1969). He quickly joined national BBC radio in London, and went on to anchor Sport on Two and Sports Report (1969–1978) on BBC Radio 2. From 1974 to 1976, he co-presented the Today programme on BBC Radio 4 on three mornings each week. He was also the radio boxing commentator for 20 years. Des Lynam moved to television in 1977 starting off with Sportswide as part of Nationwide continuing until the series ended in 1983, and then presented Grandstand. Lynam moved from the BBC to ITV in August 1999, to present ITV's live football coverage, including coverage of the midweek UEFA Champions League. Lynam continued to present football coverage for ITV until 2004. He decided to retire from presenting live sport after the Euro 2004 football championships. From 2011 to 2013, Lynam co-hosted with Christopher Matthew three series of Touchline Tales on BBC Radio 4, a humorous look at sport.

Gerard Marsden MBE born 24th September 1942 and sadly passed away on the 3rd January 2021. He was an English singer-songwriter, musician and television personality, best known for being leader of the Merseybeat band Gerry and the Pacemakers. He was the younger brother of fellow band member Freddie Marsden. Gerry and the Pacemakers formed in 1959, they were the second group signed by Brian Epstein, the first being the Beatles. Their first single was 1963's "How Do You Do It?", recommended by George Martin after it was initially given to the Beatles. This was the first number one hit for the Pacemakers. The group's second number one was "I Like It", followed by "You'll Never Walk Alone", both released later in 1963. In 2020, during the COVID-19 pandemic, he released a version of "You'll Never Walk Alone" in tribute to the National Health Service. In September 2003, Marsden had triple bypass heart surgery. He had a second heart operation in 2016. Marsden died on the 3rd January 2021 at Arrowe Park Hospital in Merseyside, after being diagnosed with a blood infection in his heart.

Robert William Hoskins born 26th October 1942 and died on the 29th April 2014 and was an English actor. His first major television role was in On the Move (1975–1976), an educational drama series directed by Barbara Derkow intended to tackle adult illiteracy. In 1983 Hoskins voiced an advert for Weetabix and during the late 1980s and early 1990s, he appeared in advertising for British Gas and British Telecom. British films such as The Long Good Friday (1980) and Mona Lisa (1986) won him the wider approval of critics, the latter film winning him a Cannes Award, Best Actor Golden Globe, BAFTA Awards, and an Academy Award nomination for Best Actor. A high point in his career was portraying private investigator Edward "Eddie" Valiant in the live-action/animated family blockbuster Who Framed Roger Rabbit (1988). Hoskins was not the first choice for the role; Harrison Ford, Bill Murray, and Eddie Murphy were all considered for the part. In August 2012, Hoskins retired from acting after being diagnosed with Parkinson's disease in 2011. On 29 April 2014, he died of pneumonia at the age of 71.

Sir William Connolly CBE born 24th November 1942 and is a Scottish artist, musician, presenter, actor, and retired stand-up comedian. Connolly's trade, in the early 1960s, was that of a welder in the Glasgow shipyards, but he gave it up towards the end of the decade to pursue a career as a folk singer. In the early 1970s, Connolly made the transition from folk singer with a comedic persona to fully-fledged comedian, for which he is now best known. In 1981, John Cleese and Martin Lewis invited Connolly to appear in that year's Amnesty show, The Secret Policeman's Other Ball. The commercial success of the special US version of The Secret Policeman's Other Ball film (Miramax Films, 1982) introduced Connolly to a wider American audience, who were attracted to the film because of the presence of Monty Python members. On the 4th June 1992, Connolly performed his 25th-anniversary concert in Glasgow. Parts of the show and its build-up were documented in The South Bank Show, which aired later in the year. In 2007 and again in 2010, he was voted the greatest stand-up comic on Channel 4's 100 Greatest Stand-Ups.

DEATHS

Prince Arthur, Duke of Connaught and Strathearn (Arthur William Patrick Albert) born on the 1st May 1850 and died on the 16th January 1942. He was the seventh child and third son of Queen Victoria and Prince Albert. He served as the Governor General of Canada, the tenth since Canadian Confederation and the only British prince to do so. In 1910 he was appointed Grand Prior of the Order of St John and held this position until 1939. Arthur was educated by private tutors before entering the Royal Military Academy, Woolwich at 16 years old. Upon graduation, he was commissioned as a lieutenant in the British Army, where he served for some 40 years. After the end of his viceregal tenure, Arthur returned to the United Kingdom and there, as well as in India, performed various royal duties, while also again taking up military duties. Though he retired from public life in 1928, he continued to make his presence known in the army well into the Second World War, before his death in 1942. He was Queen Victoria's last surviving son.

Princess Alexandra of Saxe-Coburg and Gotha, VA, CI (Alexandra Louise Olga Victoria) was born on the 1st September 1878 and died on the 16th April 1942. Her father was Prince Alfred, Duke of Edinburgh, the second-eldest son of Queen Victoria of the United Kingdom and Prince Albert of Saxe-Coburg and Gotha. Her mother was Grand Duchess Maria Alexandrovna of Russia, she was the fourth child and third daughter of Alfred, Duke of Saxe-Coburg and Gotha and Grand Duchess Maria Alexandrovna of Russia. As the wife of Ernst II, she was Princess consort of Hohenlohe-Langenburg. She was a granddaughter of both Queen Victoria of the United Kingdom and Tsar Alexander II of Russia. During Alexandra's formative years, her father, occupied with his career in the Navy and later as a ruler in Coburg, paid little attention to his family. It was Alexandra's mother who was the domineering presence in their children's life. Alexandra had four siblings: Alfred, Marie, Victoria Melita, and Beatrice. She died in Schwäbisch Hall, Baden-Wurttemberg, Germany in 1942.

Laura Annie Willson MBE was born 15th August 1877 and died on the 17th April 1942. She was an English engineer and suffragette, who was twice imprisoned for her political activities. She was one of the founding members of the Women's Engineering Society and was the first female member of the Federation of House Builders. She became strongly involved in the trade union movement, becoming branch secretary of the Women's Labour League in Halifax in 1907. She was also a secretary of the Halifax branch of the Women's Social and Political Union which formed in January 1906. She was a joint-director of the lathe-making factory Smith Barker & Willson with her husband, which during the First World War produced munitions. In 1917, the same year the Order of the British Empire honours were instituted, she was awarded an MBE for her contribution to 'Women's Work in Munitions'. She became the first woman member of the Federation of House Builders, constructing 72 houses for workers in Halifax in 1925–26.

SPORTING EVENTS 1942

Due to World War II sporting events were hit hard in the United Kingdom

1942 County Cricket Season

All first-class cricket was cancelled in the 1940 to 1944 English cricket seasons because of the Second World War; no first-class matches were played in England after Friday, 1st September 1939 until Saturday, 19th May 1945.

Ten matches were cancelled at the end of the 1939 English cricket season due to the German invasion of Poland on 1st September and the British government's declaration of war against Germany on Sunday 3rd September.

Although eleven first-class matches were arranged during the 1945 season following the final defeat of Germany in early May, it was not until the 1946 season that normal fixtures, including the County Championship and Minor Counties Championship, could resume. In contrast with much of the First World War, it was realised in the 1940s that cricket had its part to play in terms of raising both public morale and funds for charity. Efforts were made to stage matches whenever opportunity arose, especially if a suitable number of top players could be assembled. From the summer of 1941 onwards, teams such as the British Empire Eleven toured the country raising money for war charities.

At league cricket level, playing one-day matches, many competitions continued throughout the war: e.g., the Birmingham League, the Bradford League and the Lancashire League.

One venue where it would not be possible was The Oval, which was commandeered in 1939 and quickly turned into a prisoner of war camp, except that no prisoners were ever interned there. The playing area became a maze of concrete posts and wire fences.

Lords was also due for requisition but it was spared and MCC was able to stage many public schools and representative games throughout the war. A highlight in 1940 was the one-day game in which Sir PF Warner's XI, including Len Hutton and Denis Compton (who top-scored with 73), beat a West Indies XI which included Learie Constantine and Leslie Compton (an honorary West Indian for the day).

Of the more regular wartime teams, the most famous were the British Empire XI and the London Counties XI which were established in 1940. Both played one-day charity matches, mostly in the south-east and often at Lord's. The British Empire XI was founded by Pelham Warner but featured mainly English county players. The politician Desmond Donnelly, then in the Royal Air Force, began the London Counties XI. In one match between the two, Frank Woolley came out of retirement and played against the new star batsman Denis Compton. The British Empire XI played between 34 and 45 matches per season from 1940 to 1944; the London Counties XI was credited with 191 matches from 1940 to 1945.

Although the teams were successful in raising money for charity, their main purpose was to help sustain morale. Many of the services and civil defence organisations had their own teams, some of them national and featuring first-class players.

County clubs encouraged their players to join the services but at the same time pleaded with their members to continue subscriptions "as an investment for the future". While some counties (notably Somerset and Hampshire) closed for the duration, others did arrange matches. Nottinghamshire played six matches at Trent Bridge in 1940 and Lancashire mooted a scheme for a regionalised county competition to include the minor counties, but it was not taken further.

The Masters 1942

The 1942 Masters Tournament was the ninth Masters Tournament, held April 9–13 at Augusta National Golf Club in Augusta, Georgia.

Byron Nelson, the 1937 champion, won an 18-hole playoff by one stroke over runner-up Ben Hogan. Down by three strokes after four holes, Nelson played the final fourteen holes at five-under-par to claim the winner's share of $1,500 from a $5,000 purse. The playoff was refereed by tournament host Bobby Jones. Nelson was the second to win a second Masters, joining Horton Smith. On Sunday, Nelson started the final round with a three-stroke lead, with a gallery of 6,000 on the grounds. Hogan birdied 18 to shoot 70 (−2) and 280 (−8) and waited for Nelson to finish the last three holes. Nelson found a greenside bunker at 17 and bogeyed to fall into a tie. He had a 12-foot (3.7 m) birdie putt to win on the 72nd hole, but left it short and tapped in to force the Monday playoff.

It was the second playoff at the Masters; the first in 1935 was 36 holes.
This was the last Masters until 1946; it was not played from 1943 to 1945, due to World War II.

Place	Player	Country	Score	To par	Money ($)
T1	Byron Nelson	United States	68-67-72-73=280	−8	Playoff
	Ben Hogan	United States	73-70-67-70=280		
3	Paul Runyan	United States	67-73-72-71=283	−5	600
4	Sammy Byrd	United States	68-68-75-74=285	−3	500
5	Horton Smith	United States	67-73-74-73=287	−1	400
6	Jimmy Demaret	United States	70-70-75-75=290	+2	300
T7	Dutch Harrison	United States	74-70-71-77=292	+4	200
	Lawson Little	United States	71-74-72-75=292		
	Sam Snead	United States	78-69-72-73=292		
T10	Chick Harbert	United States	73-73-72-75=293	+5	100
	Gene Kunes	United States	74-74-74-71=293		

Playoff

Place	Player	Country	Score	To par	Money ($)
1	Byron Nelson	United States	69	−3	1,500
2	Ben Hogan	United States	70	−2	800

Cheltenham Gold Cup 1942

Medoc II was a French-bred, British-trained Thoroughbred racehorse who won the 1942 Cheltenham Gold Cup. He won races at the Cheltenham Festival in 1938, 1940 and 1941 before defeating a strong field in the Gold Cup but his later career was severely limited by wartime restrictions. The 1942 Gold Cup was run in front of a sparse crown in cold foggy conditions although any mention of the weather was omitted in the BBC Radio commentary in case the reports gave information to the enemy. Despite the conditions, the twelve-runner field was a strong one, containing as it did the previous winners Roman Hackle and Poet Prince. Red Rower was made the 3/1 favourite, with Medoc, ridden by Frenchie Nicholson, second choice in the betting on 9/2. Medoc was in fourth place when the complexion of the race changed completely at the final ditch: the leader Solarium fell, bringing down Broken Promise and severely hampering Red Rower. Left with a clear lead, Medoc stayed on well to win by eight lengths from Red Rower, who was in turn four lengths clear of Schubert.

2,000 Guineas

Big Game was tried over seven furlongs in a race at Salisbury and won impressively in a course record time. He was then moved up to one mile for the 2000 Guineas which was run that year on Newmarket's July course rather than the adjoining Rowley Mile. Travel restrictions, which meant that spectators had to walk several miles to reach the course, did not prevent a large attendance. Ridden by Richards, Big Game was made 8/11 favourite against thirteen opponents. He raced just behind the leaders before taking the lead from Ujiji two furlongs from the finish and going clear in the closing stages to win easily by four lengths from Watling Street and Gold Nib. The first "Royal" win in the race since Minoru in 1909 was reportedly received with "such cheering as had not before been heard in the venerable history of Newmarket" despite the fact that the King himself was not present.

St Leger

Sun Chariot was a thoroughbred racehorse who achieved the English Fillies Triple Crown by winning the 1,000 Guineas, the Oaks, and the St. Leger in 1942. She was bred by the National Stud and raced for King George VI. Sun Chariot was a filly of great talent but very difficult temperament. Before she ever appeared on a racecourse, she displayed such a lack of promise that she was nearly returned to Ireland, where the stud then was. She topped the Free Handicap after winning the Middle Park Stakes, Queen Mary Stakes and two other races. However, in her first start as a three-year-old, she refused to make any effort and was beaten for what turned out to be the only time. She won the 1,000 Guineas, Oaks (despite steering a most wayward course) and the St. Leger, in which she beat the Derby winner, Watling Street.

The Derby

Watling Street (1939–1953) was a British Thoroughbred racehorse and sire. In a career which lasted from spring 1941 to September 1942 he ran nine times and won four races. Having been rated the third best British two-year-old of his generation he went on to greater success as a three-year-old the following year when he won a wartime substitute version of The Derby and finished second in both the 2000 Guineas and the "New" St Leger. At the end of 1942 he was retired to a stud career of limited importance.

BOOKS PUBLISHED IN 1942

Five on a Treasure Island (published in 1942) is a popular children's book by Enid Blyton. It is the first book in The Famous Five series. The first edition of the book was illustrated by Eileen Soper. When siblings Julian, Dick and Anne cannot go for their usual summer holiday to Polseath, they are invited to spend the summer with their Aunt Fanny and Uncle Quentin at their home Kirrin Cottage, in the coastal village of Kirrin. They also meet their cousin Georgina, a surly, difficult girl, who tries hard to live like a boy and only answers to the name George. Despite an uncomfortable start, the cousins become firm friends and George introduces them to her beloved dog Timothy (Timmy), who secretly lives with the fisher boy, Alf, in the village as George's parents will not allow her to keep Timmy. On their way to Kirrin Island, George shows her cousins a shipwreck, explaining it was her great-great-great grandfather's ship. He had been transporting gold when the ship was wrecked in a storm, but despite divers investigating the wreck, the gold was never found. After visiting the wreck, the five arrive on the Island and are exploring the ruined castle when a huge storm blows up, making it too dangerous for them to return to the mainland. While they take shelter on the island, the sea throws up the old shipwreck, grounding it on the rocks surrounding the island.

The Body in the Library is a work of detective fiction by Agatha Christie and first published in the US by Dodd, Mead and Company in February 1942 and in UK by the Collins Crime Club in May of the same year. The maid at Gossington Hall wakes Mrs Bantry by saying, "There is a body in the library!" Dolly Bantry then wakes her husband, Colonel Arthur Bantry to go downstairs. He finds the dead body of a young woman on the hearth rug in the library, dressed up and with platinum blonde hair. The Colonel calls the police, and Mrs Bantry calls her old friend, Miss Marple. The police investigators include Colonel Melchett and Inspector Slack. Trying to identify this dead young woman, Melchett heads to the nearby cottage of Basil Blake, but Dinah Lee, a platinum blonde, arrives while Colonel Melchett is present, very much alive. Dr Haydock's autopsy reveals that the young woman, healthy but not fully matured, died between 10 pm and 12 midnight the previous evening, had been drugged and then strangled, and was not molested. Miss Marple notices that the appearance of this girl is not right, from her fingernails to her old dress. She shares this with Dolly. Hotel guest Conway Jefferson reports Ruby Keene, an 18-year-old dancer at the Majestic Hotel in Danemouth as missing. Josie Turner, employee at the hotel, identifies the body as her cousin Ruby.

Five Little Pigs is a work of detective fiction by British writer Agatha Christie, first published in the US by Dodd, Mead and Company in May 1942 under the title of Murder in Retrospect and in UK by the Collins Crime Club in January 1943 although some sources state that publication occurred in November 1942. The UK first edition carries a copyright date of 1942 and retailed at eight shillings. The book features Hercule Poirot. Five Little Pigs is unusual in the way that the same events are retold from the viewpoints of five people present on the day of the murder sixteen years earlier.

The novel was received positively at the time of publication. The "author's uncanny skill. The answer to the riddle is brilliant." and its "smashing last-minute showdown(s) . . .well up to the standard" sum up the reactions of two reviewers. Another said the author presented a "very pretty problem for the ingenious reader" and felt that the clue to the solution was "completely satisfying". Later reviewers used stronger terms of praise, of "the-murder-in-the-past plot" as being the best of Christie's use of that device, and "All in all, it is a beautifully tailored book, rich and satisfying" and possibly her best novel.[6] The solution of the mystery was "not only immediately convincing but satisfying as well, and even moving in its inevitability and its bleakness."

THE QUEEN OF MYSTERY

Agatha Christie

FIVE LITTLE PIGS

A Hercule Poirot Mystery

Previously published as MURDER IN RETROSPECT

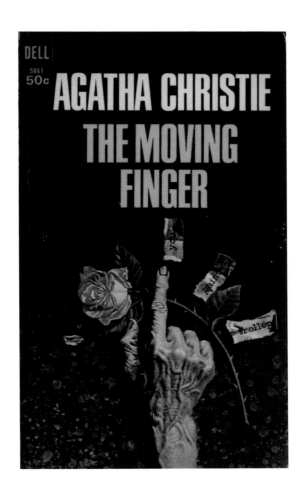

DELL
5861
50c
AGATHA CHRISTIE
THE MOVING FINGER

The Moving Finger is a detective novel by British writer Agatha Christie, first published in the USA by Dodd, Mead and Company in July 1942 and in the UK by the Collins Crime Club in June 1943. The US edition retailed at $2.00 and the UK edition at seven shillings and sixpence (7/6).

The Burtons, brother and sister, arrive in the small town (or village) of Lymstock in Devon, and soon receive an anonymous letter accusing them of being lovers, not siblings. They are not the only ones in the village to receive such letters. A prominent resident is found dead with one such letter found next to her. This novel features the elderly detective Miss Marple in a relatively minor role, "a little old lady sleuth who doesn't seem to do much". She enters the story in the final quarter of the book, in a handful of scenes, after the police have failed to solve the crime.

The novel was well received when it was published: "Agatha Christie is at it again, lifting the lid off delphiniums and weaving the scarlet warp all over the pastel pouffe." One reviewer noted that Miss Marple "sets the stage for the final exposure of the murderer." Another said this was "One of the few times Christie gives short measure, and none the worse for that." The male narrator was both praised and panned.

Four Quartets is a set of four poems written by T. S. Eliot that were published over a six-year period. The first poem, Burnt Norton, was published with a collection of his early works (1936's Collected Poems 1909–1935.) After a few years, Eliot composed the other three poems, East Coker, The Dry Salvages, and Little Gidding, which were written during World War II and the air-raids on Great Britain. They were first published as a series by Faber and Faber in Great Britain between 1940 and 1942 towards the end of Eliot's poetic career (East Coker in September 1940, Burnt Norton in February 1941, The Dry Salvages in September 1941 and Little Gidding in 1942.) The poems were not collected until Eliot's New York publisher printed them together in 1943.

Little Gidding was started after The Dry Salvages but was delayed because of Eliot's declining health and his dissatisfaction with early drafts of the poem. Eliot was unable to finish the poem until September 1942. Like the three previous poems of the Four Quartets, the central theme is time and humanity's place within it. Each generation is seemingly united and the poem describes a unification within Western civilisation. When discussing World War II, the poem states that humanity is given a choice between the bombing of London or the Holy Spirit.

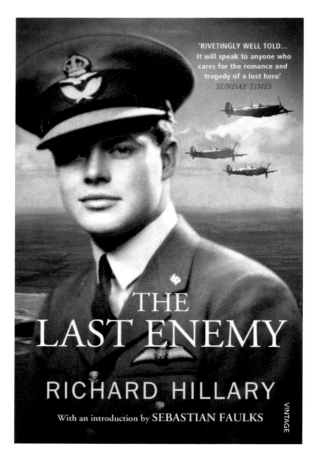

The Last Enemy (first published in America as Falling Through Space), is a war memoir written by the Second World War Anglo-Australian fighter pilot Richard Hillary detailing his experiences during the Battle of Britain in 1940.

Hillary joined the Royal Air Force at the start of the Second World War as a university undergraduate. Its text details his experiences as a Spitfire pilot during the Battle of Britain, during which he was shot down in action, sustaining severe injuries.

He wrote the book in New York City whilst still recuperating from his wounds during a propaganda publicity tour in the United States in 1941 organized by the British Government to attempt to raise support for the Allied cause and the U.S.A.'s entry into the war. However, he was not allowed to appear in public personally due to concerns that his severely facially scarred appearance might prove counter-productive, and his work was confined to newspaper interviews and radio broadcasts.

Hillary was killed in his 24th year whilst piloting an aircraft in a training accident in 1943.

The Screwtape Letters, Lewis imagines a series of lessons in the importance of taking a deliberate role in Christian faith by portraying a typical human life, with all its temptations and failings, seen from devils' viewpoints. Screwtape holds an administrative post in the bureaucracy ("Lowerarchy") of Hell, and acts as a mentor to his nephew Wormwood, an inexperienced (and incompetent) tempter. In the 31 letters which constitute the book, Screwtape gives Wormwood detailed advice on various methods of undermining God's words and of promoting abandonment of God in "the Patient" (whom Wormwood is tempting), interspersed with observations on human nature and on the Bible. In Screwtape's advice, selfish gain and power are seen as the only good, and neither demon can comprehend God's love for man or acknowledge human virtue. Versions of the letters were originally published weekly in the Anglican periodical The Guardian, in wartime between May and November 1941 and the standard edition contains an introduction explaining how the author chose to write his story. Lewis wrote the sequel "Screwtape Proposes a Toast" in 1959 – a critique of certain trends in British public education. (Although Britain calls its major private schools "public schools", Lewis is referring to state schools when he criticizes "public education".) Omnibus editions with a new preface by Lewis were published by Bles in 1961 and by Macmillan in 1962.

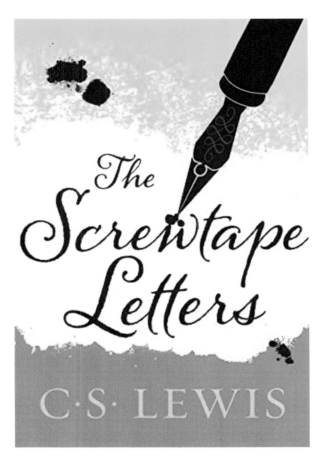

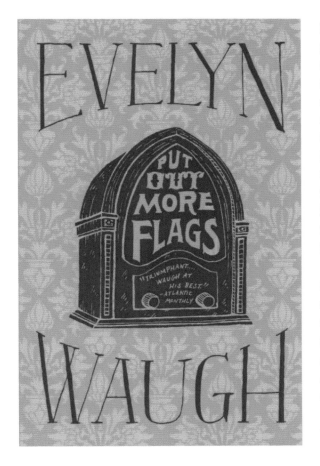

Put Out More Flags is the sixth novel by Evelyn Waugh, was first published by Chapman and Hall in 1942. At the country estate of Malfrey, Barbara Sothill loses her servants, who go off to work in factories, and her husband, who re-joins his reserve regiment. As district billeting officer, she has to find accommodation for evacuees. Her widowed mother in London tries to find an army commission for Barbara's wayward brother Basil Seal, who is sleeping with a Marxist artist called Poppet Green, but Basil fails his interview spectacularly. An aesthete friend of his, the left-wing gay Jewish intellectual Ambrose Silk, looks for a safe niche in the Ministry of Information. Basil's former mistress, the married millionairess Angela Lyne, returns from a solitary holiday in France.

Basil decides to spend the winter quietly in the country with his sister at Malfrey, where he helps her in homing problem children and then gets people to pay him for taking them away again. He meets a lonely bride whose husband is away in the army and sleeps happily with her. Back in London his friend Alastair Trumpington, refusing to try for a commission, joins the army as a private. All alone, her estranged husband Cedric having joined the army, Angela Lyne stays in her flat and takes to the bottle.

Casablanca. In World War II Casablanca, Rick Blaine, exiled American and former freedom fighter, runs the most popular nightspot in town. The cynical lone wolf Blaine comes into the possession of two valuable letters of transit. When Nazi Major Strasser arrives in Casablanca, the sycophantic police Captain Renault does what he can to please him, including detaining a Czechoslovak underground leader Victor Laszlo. Much to Rick's surprise, Lazslo arrives with Ilsa, Rick's one time love. Rick is very bitter towards Ilsa, who ran out on him in Paris, but when he learns she had good reason to, they plan to run off together again using the letters of transit. Well, that was their original plan....

Box Office

Budget: $950,000 (estimated)
Opening Weekend USA: $181,494
Gross USA: $4,108,411
Cumulative Worldwide Gross: $4,376,287

Run time is 1h 42mins

Trivia

Many of the actors who played the Nazis were in fact German Jews who had escaped from Nazi Germany.

Rick's Cafe was one of the few original sets built for the film, the rest were all recycled from other Warner Brothers productions due to wartime restrictions on building supplies.

During production, Humphrey Bogart was called to the studio to stand in the middle of the Rick's Cafe set and nod. He had no idea what the nod meant in the story--that he was giving his O.K. for the band in the cafe to play the "Marseillaise."

Rick never says "Play it again, Sam." He says: "You played it for her, you can play it for me. If she can stand it, I can. Play it!" The incorrect line has become the basis for spoofs in movies such as A Night in Casablanca (1946) and Play It Again, Sam (1972).

Goofs

Rick lets Louis into the cafe to catch Laszlo and as they walk past the first table the shadow of the microphone moves across the tabletop.

In the opening, Rick is at the back of his cafe, playing chess with himself. During a closeup of his hand, he is wearing a wedding ring. Rick is a bachelor.

When Rick and Sam get on the train after standing in the rain, their coats are completely dry.

Early on in the movie, Sam has his piano facing towards the band. A few moments later, the piano faces away from the band.

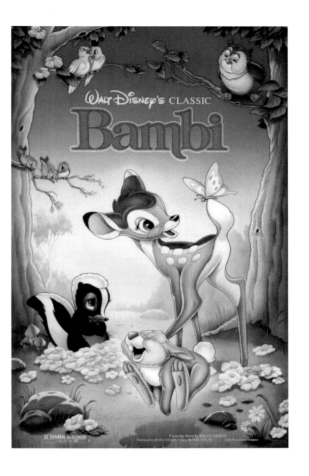

Bambi. It's spring, and all the animals of the forest are excited by the forest's latest birth, a buck fawn his mother has named Bambi. The animals are more excited than usual as Bambi's lineage means he will inherit the title of prince of the forest. Along with his mother, Bambi navigates through life with the help of his similarly aged friends, Thumper, a rabbit kit who needs to be continually reminded by his mother of all the lessons his father has taught him about how to live as a rabbit properly, and Flower, a skunk kit who likes his name. As different animals, they have their own issues and challenges which may not translate to the others. Being similarly aged, Bambi, Thumper and Flower may have to experience the uncharted phases of their lives without the knowledge or wisdom unless gleaned from those who have gone through them before. Bambi has to learn early that the lives of deer and of many of the other forest animals are not without their inherent dangers, for deer especially in the beautiful albeit exposed meadow. Bambi will also find that his ascension to prince of the forest is not a guarantee as other buck deer and situations may threaten that ascension.

Run time 1h 40mins

Trivia

"Man is in the forest" was a code phrase used by Disney's employees when Walt Disney was coming down the hallway.

No matter how skilled the animator, the Disney cartoonists simply could not draw Bambi's father's antlers accurately. This was because of the very complicated perspectives required. To get around the problem, a plaster cast was made of some real antlers which was then filmed at all angles. This footage was then rotoscoped onto animation cels.

The character of Thumper (called Bobo in the first draft) does not appear in Felix Salten's original novel. He was added by Walt Disney to bring some much-needed comic relief to the script.

Some scenes of woodland creatures and the forest fire are unused footage from Pinocchio (1940).

Goofs

When Bambi sees the possums hanging upside down from a tree, they are oriented such that the shortest is hanging on the left and the longest is on the right. Bambi rotates his head to look at them. Doing this, the longest should now be on the "left". But in the film, the longest is still on the right.

When the dogs are hunting Faline through the forest, a brown dog is in front. In the close-up, the dog is right behind Faline, trying to bite her, but it is now turned grey. In the next shot, the dog is turned brown again.

When Bambi walks backwards as an attempt to get away from Faline, he's missing two hooves.

"Arsenic and Old Lace". The year is 1941. The location is a small house next to a cemetery in Brooklyn. In this house live two kind, thoughtful, sweet old ladies, Martha and Abby Brewster who have developed a very bad habit. It appears that they murder lonely old men who have some sort of religious affiliation and they consider doing it a charity. They then leave it to their bugle blowing nephew Teddy (who thinks he's Teddy Roosevelt) to take them to the Panama Canal (the cellar) and bury them. In this instance, the "poor fellow" suffers from yellow fever found in the window seat. It is another of their nephews Mortimer Brewster, a dramatic critic, who returns home only to find the man in the seat by mistake. Another nephew, Jonathon, returns to the home after years of fleeing the authorities due to his "unofficial practice" of killing people and using their faces to change his. However, the results cause him to look like Boris Karloff (this angers him upon the mention of his similarity to the actor) due to the poor craftsmanship of his German accented, alcoholic sidekick Dr. Einstein.

Box Office
Budget: $1,120,175 (estimated)

Run Time 1h 58mins

Trivia

Some 20 years before filming this movie, actress Jean Adair had helped to nurse a very sick vaudeville performer named Archie Leach back to health; by the time she was asked to reprise her Broadway "Arsenic and Old Lace" role as Aunt Martha for this film, Adair and Leach, now known as Cary Grant, were old friends.

Cary Grant considered his acting in this film to be horribly over the top and often called it his least favourite of all his movies.

Frank Capra related to the role of Mortimer in the film because, like that character, he too had an older brother who abused him as a child and grew up to be a criminal.

Ronald Reagan and Jack Benny were offered the role of Mortimer Brewster, but turned it down. Bob Hope was offered the part and was eager to do it but Paramount Pictures refused to loan him out to Warner Bros. for the project.

Goofs

As the film opens, the narration on screen tells viewers that the action begins at 3:00 PM. However, when Mortimer & Elaine go up to the window at the marriage bureau, the clerk says "Good morning, children."

A policeman named Rooney has his rank fluctuate between "Lieutenant" and "Captain" throughout the film.

Dr. Einstein stumbles and falls into the window seat in the dark. He strikes a match, and the wire that is powering the flickering light in the palm of his hand is clearly visible trailing out from his sleeve.

When Jonathan runs his thumb along the edge of the surgical knife, it does not actually touch the blade.

"To Be or Not to Be". Joseph and Maria Tura operate and star in their own theatre company in Warsaw. Maria has many admirers including a young lieutenant in the Polish air force, Stanislav Sobinski. When the Nazis invade Poland to start World War II, Sobinski and his colleagues flee to England while the Turas find themselves now having to operate under severe restrictions, including shelving a comical play they had written about Adolf Hitler. In England meanwhile, Sobinski and his friends give Professor Siletski - who is about to return to Poland - the names and addresses of their closest relatives so the professor can carry messages for them. When it's learned that Siletski is really a German spy, Sobinski parachutes into Poland and enlists the aid of the Turas and their fellow actors to get that list back.

Box Office
Gross USA: $3,270,000
Cumulative Worldwide Gross: $4,578,000

Run time 1h 39mins

Trivia

When Jack Benny's father went to see this movie, he was outraged at the sight of his son in a Nazi uniform in the first scene and even stormed out of the theatre. Jack convinced his father that it was satire, and he agreed to sit through all of it.

When war breaks out in Poland there's a scene where grave stones are destroyed by the bombing by the German forces. One of the grave stone that is shattered has the name "Benjamin Kubelsky" which is Jack Benny's birth name.

During the shooting of a scene where storm troopers marched in the street, a female visitor to the set, who had just come from Poland and had endured such scenes for real, fell into a faint.

This apparently was the only film produced by Romaine Film Corp.

Goofs

In the scene early in the movie when Carole Lombard is arguing with the play director about her dress, they begin onstage, in the Gestapo office set. At one point the director switches to a closer shot and they are suddenly backstage, facing in entirely different directions than they were onstage.

In one sequence, Professor Siletsky pulls a gun on Joseph Tura and flees, but when we next see him trying to escape, he is no longer holding the gun in his hand.

When Professor Siletsky (Stanley Ridges) first sees Maria out of his apartment, the door doesn't close properly and comes slightly ajar, producing what appears to be a momentary hesitation from Ridges before he walks away.

"Now, Voyager". Charlotte Vale had never been out from under the domination of her matronly mother, until she enters a sanitarium. Transformed into elegant, independent woman, Charlotte begins to blossom as an individual. On a cruise to South America, she meets and falls in love for the first time with a man named Jerry. for the first time, but the affair is brief, as Jerry's married. Upon her return, Charlotte confronts her mother, who dies of a heart attack. Guilt-ridden and despondent, Charlotte returns to the sanitarium, where she meets Tina a depressed young woman who begins to find happiness with her new friend, Charlotte.

The connection these 2 shares is more than friendship, as Tina's Jerry's daughter. Through her friendship with Charlotte, Tina finds happiness, and the pair go back to Charlotte's home in Boston. When Jerry sees how happy his daughter is, he leaves her with Charlotte. What about marriage for Charlotte and Jerry? "Don't ask for the moon when we have the stars."

Run time 1h 39mins

Trivia
The biggest box office hit of Bette Davis's career.

Filming went a few weeks over schedule, which in turn caused some conflicts with Casablanca (1942), which also starred Claude Rains and Paul Henreid. Rains finished work on this movie on June 3rd in 1942 and did his first scene on Casablanca (1942) at 10:30 the next morning.

Bette Davis had walked out of Warner Bros. before the making of this movie and refused to play Charlotte Vale. According to Ginger Rogers, she had been given the script to read as a replacement of Davis and was desperate to play Charlotte. Davis got wind of this and came back to the studio, playing the character that was originally intended for her. Rogers said that she "would have given anything to play Charlotte Vale - even if I did let Jack L. Warner beat me at tennis!"

Goofs
Charlotte shows Dr. Jaquith a picture of a four funnelled ship in her photo album and tells him that it is a P&O steamer. This is incorrect as no P&O liner with four funnels was ever built.

When Charlotte gets up from the table to help Tina with the pay phone in the soda fountain her mink coat is on the back of her chair. When she returns to the table a few minutes later, the mink is gone, but it reappears a few seconds later when the camera moves from Tina back to her.

When Charlotte confronts Jerry in front of the fireplace about "The most conventional, pretentious, pious speech...", a crew member is visible in the mirror of the fireplace and quickly backs out of view.
In the beginning of the movie, Charlotte's mother tells the doctor that she had three boys and then this girl. Later in the film, Charlotte asks her mother when the father was setting up a trust for the two boys, why he didn't provide a trust for her as well.

"Jungle Book". Teenaged Mowgli, who was raised by wolves, appears in a village in India and is adopted by Messua. Mowgli learns human language and some human ways quickly, though keeping jungle ideas. Influential Merchant Buldeo is bigoted against 'beasts' including Mowgli; not so Buldeo's pretty daughter, whom Mowgli takes on a jungle tour where they find a treasure, setting the evil of human greed in motion.

Academy Awards, USA 1943

Nominee Oscar	**Best Cinematography, Colour**
	W. Howard Greene
	Best Art Direction-Interior Decoration
	Vincent Korda Julia Heron
	Best Effects, Special Effects
	Lawrence W. Butler (photographic)
	William A. Wilmarth (sound)
	Best Music, Scoring of a Dramatic Picture
	Miklós Rózsa

Run time 1h 48mins

Trivia

This was the first film for which original soundtrack recordings were issued. Previously, when record companies released music from a film, they had insisted on re-recording the music in their own studios with their own equipment. The "Jungle Book" records were taken from the same recordings used for the film's soundtrack, and their commercial success paved the way for more original-soundtrack albums.

Although Mowgli speaks to several jungle animals, only the two snakes, Father of Cobras and Kaa, respond in English. As two of the few models used to represent the animals, they were easier to control and slower than the real ones.

Mowgli's mother says he can be the Lord of the Jungle, the same title Edgar Rice Burroughs gave Tarzan, his fictional man raised by jungle animals.

Goofs

When Mowgli goes to buy the knife and is accosted by Buldeo, the position and angle of the Buldeo's rifle changes between shots. When the camera is on Mowgli, the rifle is higher than Mowgli and points to his chest; when seen from behind Mowgli, the rifle is held lower and points more to Mowgli's belly.

Two scenes with the black panther were obviously shot with the panther behind a glass screen, likely as a safeguard to protect the actors. In both scenes, showing close-ups of the panther, debris is seen adhering to the glass.

When the thieves are entering the treasure chamber, the first thief sits beside a large granite rock and begins running his hands through the gold coins. As he does so, his knee bumps the rock and it moves, showing that it is clearly just a lightweight prop.

Wires holding up the cobra in the treasure chamber can be seen.

"Cat People". Serbian national Irena Dubrovna, a fashion sketch artist, has recently arrived in New York for work. The first person who she makes a personal connection with there is marine engineer Oliver Reed. The two falls in love and get married despite Irena's reservations, not about Oliver but about herself. She has always felt different than other people, but has never been sure why. She lives close to the zoo, and unlike many of her neighbours is comforted by the sounds of the big cats emanating from the zoo. And although many see it purely as an old wives' tale, she believes the story from her village of ancient residents being driven into witchcraft and evil doing, those who managed to survive by escaping into the mountains. After seeing her emotional pain, Oliver arranges for her to see a psychiatrist to understand why she believes what she does. In therapy, Dr. Judd, the psychiatrist, learns that she also believes, out of that villagers' tale, that she has descended from this evil - women who change into great cats like panthers in passion, anger or jealousy - and that she will turn into a such a dangerous big cat upon being kissed in turn killing her lover and others who have betrayed her.

Run time 1h 13mins

Trivia

The horror movie technique of slowly building tension to a jarring shock which turns out to be something completely harmless and benign became known as a "Lewton bus" after a famous scene in this movie created by producer Val Lewton. The technique is also referred to as a "cat scare," as off-screen noises are often revealed to be a startled harmless cat.

Near the end of filming, two units were shooting around the clock to speed completion of the film. During the night, one unit would film the animals for the Central Park sequence, while during the day, the other unit would be working with the actors.

The Central Park Zoo set had previously been used in numerous RKO productions, including several Fred Astaire - Ginger Rogers musicals.

Goofs

Irena makes reference to the people of her village having mass, but this is only a Western Catholic term. As a Serb, she would likely be Eastern Orthodox and thus would use the term "Divine Liturgy."

When Dr. Judd leaves his cane in the apartment, he tucks it into the sofa cushions. When he returns to the apartment to retrieve it, it is leaning against the sofa.

In the opening scene, Oliver and Alice are standing together at the hot dog vendor's stand in the zoo. After the business of the discarded sketch, Alice has mysteriously disappeared.

When the shepherd arrives and finds the dead sheep, there's a live sheep sitting behind him. After a brief shot of the footprints that he's examining, the film returns to a shot of the shepherd, and the sheep is gone.

"Mrs Miniver". This is the story of an English middle-class family through the first years of World War II. Clem Miniver is a successful architect and his beautiful wife Kay is the anchor that keeps the family together. With two young children at home, Kay keeps busy in the quaint English village they call home. She is well-liked by everyone and the local station master has even named his new rose after her. When their son Vincent, Vin to everyone, comes home from Oxford for the summer he is immediately attracted to Carol Beldon, granddaughter of Lady Beldon. Their idyllic life is shattered in September 1939 when England is forced to declare war on Germany. Soon Vin is in the RAF and everyone has to put up with the hardship of war including blackouts and air raids. Mrs. Miniver has to deal with an escaped German flyer who makes his way to her home while husband Clem helps evacuate the trapped British Expeditionary Force from Dunkirk. Vin and Carol are married but their time together is to be short. Throughout it all, everyone displays strength of character in the face of tragedy and destruction.

Run time 2h 14mins

Trivia

Winston Churchill once said that this film had done more for the war effort than a flotilla of destroyers.

After completing the film, William Wyler joined the US Army and was posted to the Signal Corps. He was overseas on the night he won his first Oscar. He later revealed that his subsequent war experiences made him realize that the film actually portrayed war in too soft a light.

After first-choice Norma Shearer rejected the title role (as she refused to play a mother), Greer Garson was cast. Although she didn't want the part either, she was contractually bound to take it and won the Academy Award for her performance.

The first of two Academy Award Best Picture winners to receive nominations in all four acting categories. The other is "From Here to Eternity (1953)."

Goofs

In the first church service scene, a woman who is in front of the Miniver family begins sobbing with her face buried in her hands. In the next scene from a greater distance, the woman is standing and no longer crying.

In the radio broadcast of Lord Haw Haw, he mentions the fall of France. Then a day or so later, the boats are called out for the Dunkirk Rescue mission (Operation Dynamo). France did not fall until 2 weeks after Dunkirk.

Mr. Ballard's rose would not have survived the number of months over which the course of the story takes place until the flower show.

The Minivers' telephones are obviously American sets.

"The Ox-bow Incident". 1885. When transient cowboys Gil Carter and Art Croft return to Bridger's Wells, Nevada to connect with Gil's girlfriend Rose Mapen, they learn both that Rose has left town without a word and that the rustling situation that had been occurring in the area when they were last through town has gotten worse. This trip through town coincides with news that the unknown rustlers have killed Larry Kincaid, a well-known and well-liked local rancher, his cattle gone. Most of the men of the town want to see quick justice, and without the Sheriff available, they form an unofficial posse. Regardless, the recently deputized Butch Mapes illegally deputizes all the people - which includes Ma Grier - who want to be part of the posse, they working on a majority rules basis. Thus, in reality, this group is a lynch mob, who will kill who they believe to have killed Kincaid. Gil and Art decide to join the group solely because, as relative outsiders, they are the most likely possible candidates as the rustlers, and thus want to steer the suspicion away from themselves. Also included in the group are Major Tetley and his generally coward son Gerald Tetley

Run time 1h 15mins

Trivia

Henry Fonda was generally unhappy with the quality of the films he had to do while under contract to 20th Century-Fox. This was one of only two films from that period that he was actually enthusiastic about starring in. The other was The Grapes of Wrath (1940).

Henry Fonda's commitment to this film was partly due to his having witnessed, at age 14, the lynching of Will Brown in Omaha, NE, on September 28, 1919.

Director William A. Wellman loved the novel "The Ox-Bow Incident" and had long wanted to make it into a film, but the rights-holders insisted that he cast Mae West in any adaptation, which Wellman thought was ridiculous. Finally, Wellman bought the rights himself, and proceeded to make the film "his" way.

Goofs

During opening sequences when Fonda is at the bar, the whiskey he is drinking changes from clear to dark.

At the very end of the movie when Art and Gil get on their horses, you can see that Art steps up on something with his right foot, before he puts his other foot into the stirrup. In the next shot there is nothing for him to have stepped on.

After Major Tetley takes his own life behind the closed door to his study, a person apparently begins to open the door just before the cutaway to Tetley's son's reaction.

Juan Martinez throws a knife that lands right next to Farnley's foot. If you look closely you can see a thin wire attached to the end of the knife, indicating that first the scene was filmed with the knife being jerked backwards by the wire, then the film was played in reverse, to give the desired illusion of the knife landing at Farnley's feet.

Adventures of Captain Marvel. Brought to the White House to receive a Congressional Gold Medal from President Franklin D. Roosevelt, Broadway legend George M. Cohan reflects on his life. Flashbacks trace Cohan's rise, from a childhood performing in his family's vaudeville act to his early days as a struggling Tin Pan Alley songwriter to his overwhelming success as an actor, writer, director and producer known for patriotic songs like "Yankee Doodle Dandy," "You're a Grand Old Flag" and "Over There."

Academy Awards, USA 1943
Oscar Winner

Best Actor in a Leading Role
James Cagney
Best Sound, Recording
Nathan Levinson (Warner Bros. SSD)
Best Music of a Musical Picture
Ray Heindorf
Heinz Roemheld

Run time 2h 06mins

Trivia

Walking down the stairs at the White House, James Cagney goes into a tap dance. According to TCM, that was completely ad-libbed.

James Cagney became the first actor to win the Best Actor Academy Award for a musical performance.

James Cagney broke a rib while filming a dance scene, but continued dancing until it was completed.

Although a hugely patriotic film, production was already underway before the Japanese attack on Pearl Harbour took place.

James Cagney won his only Oscar for best actor for this movie. He was also nominated for "Angels with Dirty Faces" and for "Love Me or Leave Me".

Goofs

The song "Off the Record", performed near the end when Cohan is portraying Franklin D. Roosevelt in the musical "I'd Rather Be Right", features some morale boosting anti-Nazi lyrics. However, "I'd Rather Be Right" played on Broadway in 1937, two years before World War II broke out, and four years before the U.S. entered it.

In the "You're A Grand Old Flag" number, which supposedly takes place in the 1906 production of "George Washington Jr.," we see a group of Boy Scouts march onto the stage. The Scout Movement was founded in 1907 by Sir Robert Baden-Powell in England and wasn't founded in the United States until 1910.

During the dock scene where Cohan is singing "Give My Regards to Broadway," the S.S. Hurrah steams away with a 48-star flag astern. The Broadway play from which the song came was produced during the time when the flag had only 45 stars.

"Holiday Inn". Jim Hardy, Lila Dixon and Ted Hanover are a popular New York nightclub song and dance act, Jim primarily the "song", Ted the "dance", and Lila the bridge between the two. Jim's plan to ditch it all so that he and Lila can get married and become Midville, Connecticut farmers hits a snag when Lila, who admits she falls in love easily, decides she and Ted also love each other, and that she wants to remain in the spotlight. Lila and Ted become a duo, both professionally and personally. After a year, Jim finds that he is not cut out to be a full-time farmer, but still likes the country life. So, he decides he can have the best of both worlds by maintaining the farm, but opening it as an inn, only open as such for the fifteen holidays per year. Called Holiday Inn, it will feature holiday themed dinner shows written and starring Jim in a casual, relaxed atmosphere. Despite their auspicious initial meeting, Jim hires up and coming performer Linda Mason as the shows' leading lady, she who is happy for the break. Jim and Linda seem like they are falling for each other when Ted comes back into the picture after Lila falls in love with someone else and leaves him.

Run time 1h 40mins

Trivia

For the "drunk" dance, Fred Astaire had two drinks of bourbon before the first take and one before each succeeding take. The seventh and last take was used in the film.

The Connecticut Inn set for this film was reused by Paramount 12 years later as a Vermont Inn for the musical White Christmas (1954), also starring Bing Crosby and again with songs composed by Irving Berlin.

The first public performance of the song "White Christmas" was by Bing Crosby on his NBC radio show "The Kraft Music Hall" on Christmas Day, 1941, during the middle of shooting this film, which was released seven months later. The song went on to become one of the biggest selling songs in the history of music. This was the first of three films to feature Crosby singing "White Christmas" and featuring Irving Berlin's music.

The falling snow was made of chrysotile asbestos.

Goofs

When Jim first plays "White Christmas" with Linda at the inn, he sits down to play a piano. However, there is no piano present on the audio track.

The calendars shown for the last part of the film are from 1942, except for November, which is from 1941. The progression of calendars goes December 1940, February 1942, April 1942, July 1942, November 1941, and December 1942. This November calendar portrays the second-to-last vs. fourth Thursday Thanksgiving Day confusion, started in 1939 by presidential proclamation, and cleared up by congressional legislation in 1941 for the 1942 calendar.

The April calendar preceding Easter Parade clearly has a 31 after the 30th, though April does not have 31 days. A bunny's head hides the digit "1", but the "3" of the "31" is clearly visible.

MUSIC 1942

Artist	Single	Reached number one	Weeks at number one
1942			
Glenn Miller and His Orchestra with Tex Beneke	Chattanooga Choo Choo	27th December 1941	5
Glenn Miller and His Orchestra	A String of Pearls	7th February 1942	1
Woody Herman and His Orchestra with Woody Herman	Blues in the Night	14th February 1942	1
Glenn Miller and His Orchestra	A String of Pearls	21st February 1942	1
Glenn Miller and His Orchestra with Ray Eberle and the Modernaires	Moonlight Cocktail	28th February 1942	2
Jimmy Dorsey and His Orchestra with Bob Eberly and Helen O'Connell	Tangerine	9th May 1942	6
Harry James and His Orchestra	Sleepy Lagoon	20th June 1942	4
Kay Kyser and His Orchestra with Harry Babbitt, Julie Conway and the Group	Jingle Jangle Jingle	18th July 1942	8
Glenn Miller and His Orchestra with Tex Beneke, Marion Hutton and the Modernaires	(I've Got a Gal In) Kalamazoo	12th September 1942	7
Bing Crosby with the Ken Darby Singers and John Scott Trotter and His Orchestra	White Christmas	30th October 1942	11

The biggest Pop Artists of 1942 include:

The Andrews Sisters, Connee Boswell, Bing Crosby, Jimmy Dorsey and His Orchestra, Tommy Dorsey and His Orchestra, Benny Goodman and His Orchestra, Glen Gray and the Casa Loma Orchestra, Woody Herman and His Orchestra, Horace Heidt and His Orchestra, Harry James and His Orchestra, Spike Jones and His City Slickers, Dick Jurgens and His Orchestra, Sammy Kaye, Kay Kyser and His Orchestra, Jimmie Lunceford and His Orchestra, Freddy Martin and His Orchestra, The Merry Macs, The Glenn Miller Orchestra, Vaughn Monroe, Alvino Rey and His Orchestra, Dinah Shore, Freddie Slack and His Orchestra, Kate Smith, Charlie Spivak and His Orchestra

Glenn Miller and His Orchestra with Tex Beneke

"Chattanooga Choo Choo"

"**Chattanooga Choo Choo**" is a 1941 song written by Mack Gordon and composed by Harry Warren. It was originally recorded as a big band/swing tune by Glenn Miller and His Orchestra and featured in the 1941 movie Sun Valley Serenade. The Glenn Miller recording, RCA Bluebird B-11230-B, became the #1 song across the United States on December 7, 1941, and remained at #1 for nine weeks on the Billboard Best Sellers chart. The flip side of the single was "I Know Why (And So Do You)", which was the A side. The song opens up with the band, sounding like a train rolling out of the station, complete with the trumpets and trombones imitating a train whistle, before the instrumental portion comes in playing two parts of the main melody. The singer describes the train's route, originating from Pennsylvania Station in New York and running through Baltimore to North Carolina before reaching Chattanooga.

Glenn Miller and His Orchestra

"A String of Pearls"

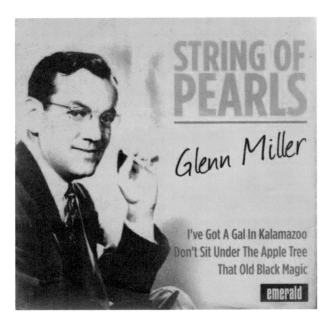

"**A String of Pearls**" is a 1941 song composed by Jerry Gray with lyrics by Eddie DeLange. It was notably recorded by Glenn Miller and His Orchestra on RCA Bluebird that November, becoming a #1 hit. The song is a big band and jazz standard. Glenn Miller and His Orchestra recorded "A String of Pearls" on the 8th November 1941 in New York, which was copyrighted and published by The Mutual Music Society, Inc., ASCAP. It was released as an RCA Bluebird 78 single, B-11382-B, backed with "Day Dreaming", in 1941 by Glenn Miller and His Orchestra. "Day Dreaming" was the A side. It became number one on the 7th February and again on the 21st for another week.

The song was featured in the 1953 Glenn Miller biopic The Glenn Miller Story starring James Stewart and also the Glenn Miller recording was featured in the 1993 comedy film Dennis the Menace starring Walter Matthau and Mason Gamble.

Woody Herman and His Orchestra

"Blues in the Night"

"Blues in the Night" is a popular blues song which has become a pop standard and is generally considered to be part of the Great American Songbook. The music was written by Harold Arlen, the lyrics by Johnny Mercer, for a 1941 film begun with the working title Hot Nocturne, but finally released as Blues in the Night. In 1942 "Blues in the Night" was one of nine songs nominated for the Academy Award for Best Original Song. Observers expected that either "Blues in the Night" or "Chattanooga Choo Choo" would win, so that when "The Last Time I Saw Paris" actually won, neither its composer, Jerome Kern, nor lyricist, Oscar Hammerstein II, was present at the ceremony. The Woody Herman recording was released by Decca Records as catalogue number 4030. The record first reached the Billboard magazine charts on the 2nd January 1942 and lasted 11 weeks on the chart, peaking at #1.

Glenn Miller and His Orchestra with Ray Eberle and the Modernaires

"Moonlight Cocktail"

"Moonlight Cocktail" is a 1942 big band song recorded by Glenn Miller during World War II. The music was composed by Luckey Roberts with lyrics by Kim Gannon. The song was originally recorded by Glenn Miller and his Orchestra on December 8, 1941, the day after the attack on Pearl Harbour. The song had its first public performance in January 1942 on WABC radio in New York City. It was the best-selling record for ten weeks, from the 28th February 1942 to the 2nd May 1942 and was the number two record for that year after Bing Crosby's "White Christmas". During World War II, the BBC initiated a program called "Victory Through Harmony" that sought to use musical radio broadcasts to maintain wartime morale and increase weapons production. Some types of music were seen as a hindrance to such goals. Along with many other popular songs of the era, "Moonlight Cocktail" was banned by the BBC as "sentimental slush" in August 1942.

Jimmy Dorsey and His Orchestra with Bob Eberly and Helen O'Connell

"Tangerine"

"**Tangerine**" is a popular song. The music was written by Victor Schertzinger, the lyrics by Johnny Mercer. It was introduced to a broad audience in the 1942 movie, The Fleet's In, produced by Paramount Pictures. The most popular recorded version of the song was made by the performers who introduced it in the film: The Jimmy Dorsey Orchestra with vocalists Helen O'Connell and Bob Eberly. The recording was released in January 1942 by Decca Records as catalogue number 4123. The record first reached the Billboard charts on the 10th April 1942, and lasted 15 weeks on the chart, including six weeks at #1. The lyrics in this version differ slightly from those in the movie. On the record, Eberly sings "And I've seen toasts to Tangerine / Raised in every bar across the Argentine," the lyric that became standard. In the movie at that point, the line is "And I've seen times when Tangerine / Had the bourgeoisie believing she were queen."

Harry James and his Orchestra

"Sleepy Logon"

"**Sleepy Logon**" The song, "Sleepy Lagoon", was published as a Lawrence-Coates collaboration in 1940. Lawrence showed the song to bandleader Harry James, whose recording of it was released by Columbia Records as catalogue number 36549. It first reached the Billboard Best Seller chart on the 17th April 1942 and lasted 18 weeks on the chart, peaking at number 1. Other hit versions were recorded by Dinah Shore, David Rose, Fred Waring, Glenn Miller and others. A recording with Tom Jenkins and his Palm Court Orchestra was made in London on the 15th March 1949. It was released by EMI on the His Master's Voice label as catalogue number B 9768. Peter Kreuder recorded the tune in 1949. The song made the Billboard Hot 100 in 1960, in a version by the Platters, found originally on the flipside of the 1960 top ten "Harbour Lights".

Kay Kyser and His Orchestra with Harry Babbitt, Julie Conway and the Group

"Jingle Jangle Jingle"

"Jingle Jangle Jingle" also known as 'I've Got Spurs That Jingle Jangle Jingle", is a song written by Joseph J. Lilley and Frank Loesser, and published in 1942. It was featured in that year's film The Forest Rangers, in which it was sung by Dick Thomas. The most commercially successful recording was by Kay Kyser, whose version reached no. 1 in the Billboard charts in July 1942.

The song was featured in the 1943 World War II-era theatrical Popeye the Sailor short Too Weak to Work,[6] and was also sung by The Sportsmen Quartet: Bill Days (top tenor), Max Smith (second tenor), Mart Sperzel (baritone), and Gurney Bell (bass) in the 1942 Western movie Lost Canyon with Hopalong Cassidy (Bill Boyd).

Glenn Miller and His Orchestra with Tex Beneke, Marion Hutton and the Modernaires

"(I've Got a Gal In) Kalamazoo"

"(I've Got a Gal in) Kalamazoo" is a #1 popular song recorded by Glenn Miller and His Orchestra in 1942. It was written by Mack Gordon and Harry Warren and published in 1942. It was featured in the musical film Orchestra Wives and was recorded by Glenn Miller and His Orchestra, featuring Tex Beneke, Marion Hutton and The Modernaires, who released it as an A side 78 in 1942, 27934-A. The B side was "At Last". The song popularized the city of Kalamazoo, Michigan. Although originally recorded by the Glenn Miller band with Tex Beneke on lead vocals, it was recreated by the fictional Gene Morrison Orchestra performing as the Glenn Miller Band and the Nicholas Brothers in the 1942 20th Century Fox movie Orchestra Wives. The song was nominated for Best Music, Original Song at the Academy Awards. The Glenn Miller record was the year's best-selling recording.

Bing Crosby with the Ken Darby Singers and John Scott Trotter and His Orchestra

"White Christmas"

"White Christmas" Bing Crosby recorded a version of the song for release as a single with the Kim Darby Singers and the John Scott Trotter Orchestra on the 29th May 1942 - a few months before the movie hit theatres. At the advice of Bing's record producer Jack Kapp, this original first verse was excised as it made no sense outside of the context of the film. Now starting with the familiar, "I'm dreaming of a white Christmas," the song became a huge hit, going to #1 on the Billboard chart in October, and staying in the top spot for 11 weeks, taking it through the first two weeks of 1943. The song enjoyed a sales resurgence every Christmas after it was first released in 1942. It went to #1 that year in America, and again reached the top spot in 1945 and 1947. The song appeared on various Billboard charts every year until 1963 when it finally dropped off the Hot 100.

Alton Glenn Miller was an American big-band trombonist, arranger, composer, and bandleader in the swing era. He was the best-selling recording artist from 1939 to 1942, leading one of the best-known big bands. Miller's recordings include "In the Mood", "Moonlight Serenade", "Pennsylvania 6-5000", "Chattanooga Choo Choo", "A String of Pearls", "At Last", "(I've Got a Gal In) Kalamazoo", "American Patrol", "Tuxedo Junction", "Elmer's Tune", and "Little Brown Jug". In just four years Glenn Miller scored 16 number-one records and 69 top ten hits—more than Elvis Presley (38 top 10s) and the Beatles (33 top 10s) did in their careers. While he was traveling to entertain U.S. troops in France during World War II, Miller's aircraft disappeared in bad weather over the English Channel.

WORLD EVENTS 1942

January

1st | The Declaration by United Nations is signed by China, the United Kingdom, the United States, the Soviet Union, and 22 other nations, in which they agree "not to make any separate peace with the Axis powers".

2nd | The United States Eighth Air Force is activated in Savannah, Georgia.

7th | Operation Typhoon, the German attempt to take Moscow, ends in failure. The Battle of Moscow was a military campaign that consisted of two periods of strategically significant fighting on a 600 km (370 mi) sector of the Eastern Front during World War II. It took place between October 1941 and January 1942. The Soviet defensive effort frustrated Hitler's attack on Moscow, the capital and largest city of the Soviet Union. Moscow was one of the primary military and political objectives for Axis forces in their invasion of the Soviet Union.

11th | Dutch East Indies campaign: Japan declares war on the Netherlands and invades the Dutch East Indies.

13th | Henry Ford patents a plastic automobile which would be 30% lighter than a regular car. The project culminated in 1942, when Ford patented an automobile made almost entirely of plastic, attached to a tubular welded frame. It weighed 30% less than a steel car and was said to be able to withstand blows ten times greater than steel. It ran on grain alcohol (ethanol) instead of gasoline. The design never caught on.

14th | WWII: "Second Happy Time", the German submarine commanders' name for Operation Paukenschlag (Operation Drumbeat), the phase in the Battle of the Atlantic during which German submarines are successful in attacking Allied shipping along the East Coast of the United States, opens early this morning when German submarine U-123 under the command of Reinhard Hardegen sinks a Norwegian tanker within sight of Long Island, before entering New York Harbour and sinking a British tanker off Sandy Hook the following night, as she leaves heading south along the coast. U-boat successes continue until around 12th June.

16th | American film actress Carole Lombard and her mother are among all 22 killed aboard TWA Flight 3 when the Douglas DC-3 plane crashes into Potosi Mountain near Las Vegas while she is returning from a tour to promote the sale of war bonds.

19th | Japanese forces invade Burma.

January

20th Senior Nazi officials met at the Wannsee Conference to agree on the implementation of the Final Solution, whereby Jews in German-occupied territories would be deported to Poland and systematically murdered in extermination camps.

21st One Heinkel He 111 medium bomber raided the Free French-controlled Fort Lamy in French Equatorial Africa. The plane bombed the fort unchallenged but then ran low on fuel and had to make an emergency landing, leaving the crew stranded some 120 miles from their airstrip in southern Libya until a Junkers Ju 52 transport aircraft arrived a week later with fuel.

22nd 5,300 Japanese troops commanded by Major General Tomitarō Horii steamed into Rabaul Harbour during the night.

24th A committee assigned by President Roosevelt on the 18th December 1941 to investigate the Pearl Harbour attack issued its report, putting the blame on Admiral Husband E. Kimmel and Lieutenant General Walter Short for failing to coordinate their defences appropriately or taking measures reasonably required in the light of the warnings they had been given. Both men would receive death threats as a result of the report.

26th The first American soldiers to land in the European theatre of operations disembarked at Belfast, Northern Ireland. Their arrival was kept a secret right up until the first ship docked.

27th Japanese submarine I-73 was torpedoed and sunk 240 miles west of Midway Atoll by the USS Gudgeon. This marked the first time in the war that a United States Navy submarine sank an enemy warship.

30th Rommel retook Benghazi by noon. Just as he entered the city, he received a message from Benito Mussolini suggesting that he should launch an offensive to take Benghazi. Rommel sent back a curt response: "Benghazi already taken." 1,000 men of the 4th Indian Division were still trapped in the city and surrendered when it fell.

31st The German cargo ship MV Spreewald was mistaken for a British ship, torpedoed and sunk north of the Azores by German submarine U-333.

February

1st National Freedom Day was observed for the first time in the United States, commemorating Abraham Lincoln's signing of the Thirteenth Amendment to the U.S. Constitution on the 1st February 1865.

2nd The drama film Kings Row starring Ann Sheridan, Robert Cummings and Ronald Reagan premiered in New York City.

3rd Erwin Rommel's forces captured Timimi in Libya. The British Eighth Army fell back and began establishing what would soon be known as the Gazala Line.

5th The Canadian troopship RMS Empress of Asia was sunk by Japanese dive bombers near Singapore.

7th Rommel halted his counteroffensive near Gazala. In a little over two weeks, he had retaken almost all the ground that the British Eighth Army had taken at the end of 1941.

8th The Demyansk Pocket was created when a pocket of German troops was encircled by the Red Army around Demyansk south of Leningrad.

February

9th The ocean liner USS Lafayette (formerly SS Normandie) capsized and sank in New York Harbour whilst under conversion to a troopship.

10th The last civilian car rolled off the assembly line at the River Rouge Ford plant before the company switched production over to military vehicles such as service trucks and jeeps. Reporters and photographers were on hand to document the event.

11th Jacob Epstein's huge new sculpture depicting the Biblical story of Jacob wrestling with the angel went on show in London. His treatment of religious subject matter in a primitivist style was controversial for its time.

13th The German Navy completed the Channel Dash, they managed to avoid British air & naval attacks, but both battlecruisers were seriously damaged by British sea mines.

14th The British Air Ministry issued the Area bombing directive, ordering RAF bombers to attack the German industrial workforce and the morale of the German populace through bombing German cities and their civilian inhabitants.

15th President Roosevelt made a special broadcast to the people of Canada. "Yours are the achievements of a great nation," the president said after reviewing Canada's part in the war effort. "They require no praise from me-but they get that praise from me nevertheless. I understate the case when I say that we, in this country, contemplating what you have done, and the spirit in which you have done it, are proud to be your neighbours."

18th Free French submarine Surcouf possibly sank north of Cristóbal, Colón, Panama after a collision with American freighter Thompson Lykes, though its fate is uncertain.

19th Bombing of Darwin: 242 Japanese aircraft attacked the harbour and airfields around Darwin, Australia. The town was lightly defended and the Japanese inflicted heavy losses. Tanker British Motorist, cargo ships Don Isidro, Mauna Loa, Meigs, Neptuna and Zealandia, coal hulk Kelat, transport ship Portmar patrol boats Coongoola and Mavie and destroyers USS Peary and HNLMS Piet Hein were all sunk. Hajime Toyoshima crash-landed on Melville Island and became the first Japanese prisoner of war on Australian soil.

20th | Edward O'Hare became the U.S. Navy's first flying ace. He single-handedly attacked a formation of nine heavy bombers approaching his aircraft carrier. Even though he had a limited amount of ammunition, he was credited with shooting down five of the enemy bombers and became the first naval recipient of the Medal of Honour in World War II.

21st | Madame Chiang Kai-shek broadcast her husband's farewell message over Indian radio. "In these horrible times of savagery and brute force, the people of China and their brethren the people of India should, for the sake of civilization and human freedom, give their united support to the principles embodied in the Atlantic Charter and in the joint declaration of the 26 nations, and ally themselves with the anti-aggression front," the message read. "I hope the Indian people will wholeheartedly join the allies-namely, China, Great Britain, America and the Soviet Union-and participate shoulder to shoulder in the struggle for survival of a free world until complete victory has been achieved and the duties incumbent upon them in these troubled times have been fully discharged."

23rd | Joseph Stalin marked the 24th anniversary of the founding of the Red Army with a statement broadcast to all Russians declaring that a "tremendous and hard fight" still ahead, but now that the Germans had spent the "element of surprise" the Soviets were taking the offensive and that "the Red banner will fly everywhere it has flown before."

24th | Voice of America began short-wave radio broadcasts. Its initial programmes were in German.

25th | A mysterious event called the Battle of Los Angeles took place in the early morning hours over Los Angeles, California when an anti-aircraft artillery barrage was fired into the night time sky. Secretary of the Navy Frank Knox called the incident a "false alarm" but offered no other information.

26th | The 14th Academy Awards were held in Los Angeles. How Green Was My Valley won Best Picture, and its director John Ford won his third Oscar for Best Director. The category Best Documentary was awarded for the first time, won by the National Film Board of Canada's entry Churchill's Island.

27th | The Battle of the Java Sea was fought in the Pacific, resulting in a Japanese victory. The Allies lost two cruisers and three destroyers while the Japanese only had a destroyer damaged in return.

28th | American destroyer Jacob Jones and tanker R.P. Resor were torpedoed and sunk east of New Jersey by German submarine U-578.

March

3rd KNILM Douglas DC-3 shootdown: A Douglas DC-3 airliner was shot down over Australia by Japanese warplanes, resulting in the deaths of four passengers and the loss of diamonds worth an estimated A£ 150,000–300,000. The diamonds were presumably looted from the crash site but their fate remains a mystery.

4th The Japanese conducted Operation K, a reconnaissance of Pearl Harbour and disruption of repair and salvage operations there. Two Kawanishi H8K flying boats were dispatched but failed to see much due to heavy clouds and only did negligible bombing damage.

6th Elements of the Japanese 2nd Infantry Division on Java entered Buitenzorg, while Dutch forces withdrew toward Bandung.

7th Netherlands Indies Radio went off the air with the final message, "Goodbye till better times. Long live the Queen!"

9th Vannevar Bush delivered a report to President Roosevelt expressing optimism on the possibility of producing an atomic bomb.

11th On the 11th March 1942, during World War II, General Douglas MacArthur and members of his family and staff left the Philippine island of Corregidor and his forces, which were surrounded by the Japanese. They travelled in PT boats through stormy seas patrolled by Japanese warships and reached Mindanao two days later. From there, MacArthur and his party flew to Australia in a pair of Boeing B-17 Flying Fortresses, ultimately arriving in Melbourne by train on 21 March. In Australia, he made his famous speech in which he declared, "I came through and I shall return".

12th Brothers Anthony and William Esposito were executed by electric chair five minutes apart at Sing Sing for the 14th January 1941 slaying of a police officer and a holdup victim, which had led to a sensational trial in which they feigned insanity. Both brothers were in such fragile health that they had to be brought into the death chamber in wheelchairs because they had refused all food for the past 10 months that was not fed them forcibly.

13th The musical comedy film Song of the Islands starring Betty Grable and Victor Mature was released.

14th U.S. President Franklin D. Roosevelt sent a proposal to all 48 state governors that speed limits throughout the nation be reduced to 40 miles per hour (64 km/h) to conserve rubber.

15th The Dünamünde Action was an operation launched by the Nazi German occupying force and local collaborationists in Biķernieki forest, near Riga, Latvia. Its objective was to execute Jews who had recently been deported to Latvia from Germany, Austria, Bohemia and Moravia. These murders are sometimes separated into the First Dünamünde Action, occurring on the 15th March 1942, and the Second Dünamünde Action on March 26, 1942. About 1,900 people were killed in the first action and 1,840 in the second. The victims were lured to their deaths by a false promise that they would receive easier work at a (non-existent) resettlement facility near a former neighbourhood in Latvia called Daugavgrīva (Dünamünde). Rather than being transported to a new facility, they were trucked to woods north of Riga, shot, and buried in previously dug mass graves. The elderly, the sick and children predominated among the victims.

March

21st | The spy film Secret Agent of Japan starring Preston Foster premiered at the Globe Theatre in New York City. It was the first film to include the attack on Pearl Harbour as part of the plot.

22nd | Cripps' mission: The British government sent Stafford Cripps to India to disclose the British constitutional proposals for a post-war India. Britain promised self-government for India after the war in exchange for their co-operation in the war effort.

23rd | Hitler issued Directive No. 40, pertaining to the command organization of the Atlantic Wall. Hitler ordered the construction of the fortifications on the 23rd March 1942. More than a half million French workers were drafted to build it. The wall was frequently mentioned in Nazi propaganda, where its size and strength were usually exaggerated. The fortifications included colossal coastal guns, batteries, mortars, and artillery, and thousands of German troops were stationed in its defences. When the Allies eventually invaded the Normandy beaches in 1944, most of the defences were stormed within hours. Today, ruins of the wall exist in all of the nations where it was built, although many structures have fallen into the ocean or have been demolished over the years.

Atlantic Wall 1942-1944

25th | Holocaust in Slovakia: The first mass transport of Jews to Auschwitz concentration camp departs from Poprad railway station in the Slovak Republic, consisting of 997 young women.

26th | Police in Rio de Janeiro announced that they had smashed a Nazi spy ring with the arrest of 200 operatives.

27th | Joe Louis knocked out Abe Simon in the sixth round at Madison Square Garden to retain the World Heavyweight Boxing Championship.

28th | Bombing of Lübeck: The port city of Lübeck was the first German city attacked in substantial numbers by the Royal Air Force. The night attack caused a firestorm that caused severe damage to the historic centre and led to the retaliatory Baedeker raids on historic British cities.

30th | The exclusion of Japanese-American internees begin in Bainbridge Island, Washington.

April

1st | Italian cruiser Giovanni delle Bande Nere was sunk off Stromboli by the British submarine HMS Urge.

2nd | The comedy film My Favourite Blonde starring Bob Hope and Madeleine Carroll was released.

4th | The Luftwaffe carried out Operation Eisstoß (Ice Assault) with the objective of smashing the Soviet fleet at Kronstadt, which was well-protected by anti-aircraft guns. 62 Stukas, 70 bombers and 50 Bf 109s were deployed and managed to inflict damage on thirteen Soviet warships, but not a single one was sunk.

5th | British Commandos attempted Operation Myrmidon, a raid on the Adour Estuary in southwest France, but the attack was called off when they encountered a sandbar that they had not expected.

7th | A devastating air raid was conducted against the Maltese capital of Valletta. The Royal Opera House, one of the most beautiful buildings in the city, took a direct hit and was reduced to rubble.

8th | The Canadian government created the Park Steamship Company to build Park ships, the Canadian equivalent of the American Liberty ships and British Fort ships.

Park Ship

Liberty Ship

Fort Ship

10th | The minesweeper USS Finch was bombed and damaged by Japanese aircraft in Manila Bay, sinking the next day.

12th | The first units of the Hungarian 2nd Army left for the Eastern Front.

13th | The Imber friendly fire incident occurred at Imber, England when a Royal Air Force fighter aircraft taking part in a firepower demonstration accidentally opened fire on a crowd of spectators, killing 25 and wounding 71.

14th | German submarine U-85 became the first casualty of Operation Drumbeat when she was sunk near Cape Hatteras by the American destroyer Roper.

17th | The main oilfields in Burma were destroyed to prevent them from falling into Japanese hands.

18th | The Toronto Maple Leaf's defeated the Detroit Red Wings 3-1 in Game 7 of the Stanley Cup Finals to complete one of the greatest comebacks in sports history. After losing the first three games of the series, the Maple Leaf's won the next four and claimed their fourth Stanley Cup in franchise history.

19th | Bernard Joseph Smith won the Boston Marathon, setting a new American record time of 2:26:51.

20th | The Allies executed Operation Calendar, the delivery of 48 Supermarine Spitfire aircraft to Malta. However, the planes were almost immediately destroyed on the ground.

April

21st | An Anglo-Canadian force conducted Operation Abercrombie, an overnight reconnaissance raid on the area around the French coastal village of Hardelot.

22nd | The Alfred Hitchcock-directed spy thriller film Saboteur starring Robert Cummings and Priscilla Lane premiered in Washington, D.C.

24th | The comedy gangster film Larceny, Inc. starring Edward G. Robinson premiered in New York City.

25th | Berlin radio announced that French general Henri Giraud had escaped from Königstein Fortress. A 100,000-mark reward was offered for information leading to his recapture.

26th | The German Reichstag convened for what would be its final session. Chancellor Adolf Hitler gave a long speech asking for total legislative and judicial power that would give him the right to promote or punish anyone with no regard to legal procedures. The Reichstag agreed and Hitler was given absolute power of life and death.

May

1st | Joseph Stalin published a message on International Workers' Day in which he stated that the Soviet Union was fighting a "patriotic war of liberation" and had no aim of "seizing foreign countries" or "conquering foreign peoples."

2nd | German submarine U-573 entered port at Cartagena, Spain for repairs after being severely damaged on the 29th April by depth charges from RAF Lockheed Hudsons. Spanish authorities granted U-573 a three-month period for repairs despite protests from the British embassy.

5th | The French submarine Bévéziers was depth charged and sunk by Swordfish torpedo bombers at Diego Suarez, Madagascar.

6th | The Battle of Corregidor ended when 10,000 U.S. and Filipino troops surrendered to the Japanese.

7th | In the Battle of the Coral Sea, Japanese aircraft carrier Shōhō and the American destroyer Sims were sunk, while the American oiler Neosho was crippled by bombing and had to be scuttled four days later.

8th | The drama film In This Our Life starring Bette Davis, Olivia de Havilland, Charles Coburn and George Brent was released.

10th | The Allies executed Operation Bowery, a repeat of the earlier Operation Calendar delivering Supermarine Spitfire fighter planes to Malta. This time, the newly arrived fighters got back into the air quickly before an air raid could destroy them.

11th | The armed naval trawler Bedfordshire was torpedoed and sunk off Ocracoke Island, North Carolina by German submarine U-558.

13th | Action of 13 May 1942: Motor Torpedo Boats of the Royal Navy attempted to stop the German auxiliary cruiser Stier from reaching Gironde, France. Although Stier made it through the English Channel, two German torpedo boats were sunk with one British MTB lost in return.

14th | U.S. intelligence partially decoded a Japanese message indicating that a large force was preparing to invade "AF". Cryptanalyst Joseph Rochefort suspected that AF represented Midway Island, but officials in Washington believed it stood for the Aleutians. The matter was settled by planting an easily readable message from Midway saying that their desalination plant had broken down. When a Japanese message was then transmitted reporting that "AF" was short of water, Rochefort's belief was confirmed.

15th | The first seventeen U.S. states put gasoline rationing into effect after it became apparent that voluntary rationing was insufficient.

17th | Red Star Olympique defeated FC Sète 2-0 in the Coupe De France Final.

18th | The biggest contingent of U.S. troops yet to arrive in Europe landed in Northern Ireland.

21st | The comedy-drama film Tortilla Flat starring Spencer Tracy, Hedy Lamarr and John Garfield was released.

22nd | Baseball star Ted Williams enlisted in the U.S. Navy aviation program.

May

23rd | Hitler gave an address to senior Nazis in which he said that concentration camps were the main bulwark against an uprising.

24th | A 15-minute test blackout centred on Detroit was held starting at 10 p.m., with neighbouring communities such as Pontiac and Windsor, Ontario also participating. It was the largest blackout in the Midwestern United States up to that time.

25th | Principal photography began on the film Casablanca.

26th | The Anglo-Soviet Treaty was signed in London, pledging twenty years of alliance and mutual assistance between the United Kingdom and the Soviet Union.

27th | Operation Anthropoid, the attempted assassination of Reinhard Heydrich, was carried out. Heydrich was only wounded but died of his injuries eight days later.

28th | Italian opera singer Ezio Pinza was released from Ellis Island after being held since March on suspicion of being an enemy alien.

29th | The biographical musical film Yankee Doodle Dandy starring James Cagney as the songwriter and entertainer George M. Cohan premiered in New York City. Instead of tickets, Warner Bros. sold war bonds to the premiere ranging from $25 to $25,000 in price.

30th | Fred Korematsu was arrested on a street corner in San Leandro, California after being identified as being of Japanese ancestry, despite plastic surgery on his eyelids in an attempt to pass for Caucasian. The legality of his internment would be taken all the way to the Supreme Court in the landmark case Korematsu v. United States.

June

1st | Adolf Hitler visited Army Group South's headquarters at Poltava to confirm plans for the upcoming summer offensive.

2nd | During the Siege of Sevastopol, the German 11th Army began a massive five-day artillery barrage on the fortress city using 620 guns including the enormous 800mm Schwerer Gustav "Dora" gun.

3rd | The Battle of Midway began. The Japanese sought to deliver another crushing blow to the U.S. Navy to ensure Japanese dominance in the Pacific, but American codebreakers had determined the time and place of the Japanese attack in advance, enabling the U.S. Navy to prepare its own ambush.

4th | Hitler paid a rare visit outside the Reich when he went to Finland to see Carl Mannerheim, ostensibly to congratulate him on his 75th birthday. Mannerheim did not want the encounter to look like an official state visit so the two met in secret near Immola Airfield. The meeting was clandestinely recorded and today it is the only known evidence of Hitler speaking in his private conversational voice.

6th | During the Battle of Midway, Japanese cruiser Mikuma was bombed and sunk by Douglas SBD Dauntless aircraft. American destroyer Hammann was torpedoed and sunk by Japanese submarine I-168.

8th | The nine-day long Attack on Sydney Harbour by Japanese submarines ended indecisively.

June

9th — A lavish funeral was held for Reinhard Heydrich in Berlin. He was posthumously awarded the German Order.

10th — The Czech village of Lidice was completely destroyed by German forces in reprisal for the assassination of Reinhard Heydrich.

12th — The Allies launched Operation Harpoon and Operation Vigorous, two simultaneous convoys sent to supply Malta. Operation Harpoon or Battle of Pantelleria was one of two simultaneous Allied convoys sent to supply Malta in the Axis-dominated central Mediterranean Sea in mid-June 1942, during the Second World War. Operation Vigorous was a westward convoy from Alexandria run at the same time Operation Harpoon was an eastbound convoy operation from Gibraltar. Two of the six ships in the Harpoon convoy completed the journey, at the cost of several Allied warships. The Vigorous convoy was driven back by the Italian fleet and attacks by Axis aircraft.

14th — The General Electric Company in Bridgeport, Connecticut finished production on the new M1 rocket launcher, commonly known as the bazooka.

16th — The war film Eagle Squadron starring Robert Stack, Diana Barrymore, John Loder and Nigel Bruce was released.

17th — Japanese Prime Minister Hideki Tojo was slightly wounded when a Korean nationalist shot him in the left arm outside the old war ministry building in Tokyo. Japanese police returned fire and killed the man identified as 31-year-old Park Soowon. The incident was not revealed to the public for two months.

18th — Charles de Gaulle gave a speech at the Royal Albert Hall in London praising the unity of the Resistance movements.

19th — A light aircraft carrying German major Joachim Reichel crash-landed on the Eastern Front behind Russian lines. Reichel was killed in the crash and documents he was carrying pertaining to the upcoming German offensive fell into Soviet hands. German High Command debated over how much to revise their plans in light of the security breach but as it turned out, Stalin believed the documents were planted by the Germans in order to deceive the Soviets and ordered them to be ignored.

20th — The comic book villain Two-Face made his first appearance in Detective Comics issue #66.

June

21st | The temperature in Tirat Zvi reaches 54 degrees Celsius (129.2 degrees Fahrenheit), for what remains the highest temperature ever recorded in Israel.

22nd | Vichy French Prime Minister Pierre Laval made a radio broadcast in which he stated, "I wish for a German victory, because, without it, Bolshevism tomorrow would settle everywhere." This speech shocked many of the French people who were still holding out hope that the Vichy regime was playing a waiting game with the Germans until France could be liberated in an Allied victory.

23rd | Hitler wrote to Benito Mussolini with "heartfelt advice" recommending that he postpone Operation Herkules and instead "order the continuation of operations to seek the complete destruction of British forces to the very limits of what your high command and Marshal Rommel think is militarily possible with their existing troops. The goddess of fortune in battle comes to commanders only once, and he who fails to seize the opportunity at such a moment will never be given a second chance." Mussolini complied with Hitler's veiled order and postponed Herkules to September.

26th | President Roosevelt signed a new law prohibiting the making of unauthorized photographs or sketches of military property such as bases or ships.

27th | The British war film One of Our Aircraft Is Missing starring Godfrey Tearle, Eric Portman and Hugh Williams was released.

28th | The Germans began Case Blue on the Eastern Front. The summer offensive opened with the Battle of Voronezh.

29th | Benito Mussolini flew to Derna, Libya in anticipation of leading a triumphal entry of Axis forces into Cairo.

30th | All remaining Jewish schools were closed in Germany.

July

1st The Japanese auxiliary ship Montevideo Maru was torpedoed and sunk off Cape Bojeador, Luzon, Philippines by the American submarine Sturgeon, unaware that it was carrying a large number of Australian prisoners of war and civilians. 1,054 Australians perished, the worst maritime disaster in Australian history.

3rd The Flying Tigers fought their final engagement, driving away eight Japanese bombers raiding Hengyang. The First American Volunteer Group (AVG) of the Republic of China Air Force in 1941–1942, nicknamed the Flying Tigers, was composed of pilots from the United States Army Air Corps (USAAC), Navy (USN), and Marine Corps (USMC), recruited under President Franklin Roosevelt's authority before Pearl Harbour and commanded by Claire Lee Chennault.

4th The 15th Bombardment Squadron became the first USAAF unit to bomb occupied Europe when it joined the RAF in a raid on the Netherlands.

6th The American League defeated the National League 3-1 in the 10th Major League Baseball All-Star Game at the Polo Grounds in New York City. It was the first night game in All-Star history.

8th One week after gaining U.S. citizenship, the British-born movie star Cary Grant married the socialite heiress Barbara Hutton at Lake Arrowhead, California.

9th Adolf Hitler modified Case Blue, dividing Army Group South into two groups. Army Group A was to seize Rostov-on-Don and then continue through the Caucusus, while Group B was to drive on Stalingrad through to Astrakhan. Hitler also ordered Hermann Hoth's forces to head south in the hope of encircling the Red Army units still west of the Don River.

11th Allied convoy PQ 17, finally arrived in Russia after losing 24 of its original 33 vessels, the worst convoy loss of the war. Joseph Stalin suspected that the British had fabricated the heavy losses so as to provide the Soviets with fewer goods than promised.

13th 5,000 Jews from the Rovno ghetto were shot in a forest near the city.

14th Two women were shot dead in Marseille when an enormous crowd gathered illegally for Bastille Day, waving French flags and singing "La Marseillaise". Charles de Gaulle led Bastille Day celebrations of his own in London.

16th A decree was published in Paris announcing that the "nearest male relatives, brothers-in-law, and cousins of troublemakers above the age of eighteen will be shot. All women relatives of the same degree of kinship will be condemned to forced labour. Children of less than eighteen years old of all the above-mentioned persons will be placed in reform schools."

19th Germany's Second Happy Time drew to a close as U-boats were ordered withdrawn from the U.S. east coast because of the increasing effectiveness of American antisubmarine measures.

22nd Grossaktion Warsaw: Mass deportations of Jews began from the Warsaw Ghetto to Treblinka.

23rd The German 1st Panzer Army captured Rostov-on-Don.

July

25th   On the 25th July 1942, German troops captured Rostov-on-Don, Russia, opening the Caucasus region of the southern Soviet Union, and the oil fields beyond at Maikop, Grozny, and ultimately Baku, to the Germans. Two days prior, Adolf Hitler issued a directive to launch such an operation into the Caucasus region, to be named Operation Edelweiß. German forces were compelled to withdraw from the area that winter as Operation Little Saturn threatened to cut them off.

28th   Arthur Harris made a radio broadcast informing German listeners that the bombers would soon be coming "every night and every day, rain, blow or snow - we and the Americans. I have just spent eight months in America, so I know exactly what is coming. We are going to scourge the Third Reich from end to end, if you make it necessary for us to do so ... it is up to you to end the war and the bombing. You can overthrow the Nazis and make peace."

30th   WAVES, the women's branch of the United States Navy Reserve, was founded in the United States.

August

1st   1942–44 musicians' strike: The American Federation of Musicians went on strike against the major U.S. recording companies because of disagreements over royalty payments.

4th   Citing documents seized in a raid on Indian National Congress headquarters in Allahabad, the British government accused Mahatma Gandhi and the majority of his party of working toward "appeasement" of Japan.

6th   For aiding an escaped German prisoner of war, Detroit restaurant owner Max Stephan became the first American sentenced to execution for treason since the Whiskey Rebellion in 1794.

8th   U.S. Marines captured the unfinished Japanese airbase on Guadalcanal. The base was named Henderson Field after the Battle of Midway hero Lofton R. Henderson.

9th   The New York Times Best Seller list switched from a local survey to a national one compiled from booksellers in 22 cities. The first Fiction Best Seller under the new system was And Now Tomorrow by Rachel Field.

10th   Japanese cruiser Kako was torpedoed and sunk off Simbari Island, New Ireland by the American submarine USS S-44.

11th   Al Milnar of the Cleveland Indians and Tommy Bridges of the Detroit Tigers had one of the most epic pitchers' duels in baseball history. With the game locked in a scoreless tie in the top of the ninth inning, Milnar lost a no-hitter with two out when Doc Cramer singled to right field. Both pitchers maintained their shutouts until the fifteenth inning when the game was finally called in a 0–0 tie.

12th   Movie star Clark Gable entered a U.S. Army recruiting station in Los Angeles and enlisted as a private at the age of 41.

13th   Japan passed the Enemy Airmen's Act, stating that Allied airmen participating in bombing raids against Japanese-held territory would be treated as "violators of the law of war" and subject to trial and punishment if captured.

August

16th In Bilbao, Spain, a mass was held at the Basilica of Begoña to commemorate members of the Begoña Regiment who died in the Civil War. After the service there was some shouting between the Falangist and Carlist factions, and during the ensuing scuffle a Falangist threw two hand grenades and wounded 30 people.

17th The USAAF made its first air raid on occupied Europe, bombing railroad marshaling yards at Sotteville-lès-Rouen.

18th 900 Japanese troops landed at Taivu Point on Guadalcanal, while another 500 landed at Kokumbona. These landings were the first run of what the U.S. Marines nicknamed the Tokyo Express.

19th The Dieppe Raid took place on the northern coast of France. The operation was virtually a complete failure and almost 60% of the 6,086 men who made it ashore were killed, wounded or captured. The British destroyer Berkeley was crippled by Focke-Wulf Fw 190s and scuttled.

20th The comedy-drama film The Talk of the Town starring Cary Grant, Jean Arthur and Ronald Colman was released.

 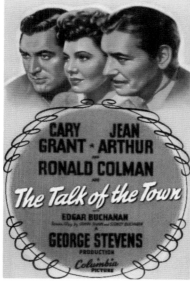 

Cary Grant   Jean Arthur

22nd Brazil declared war on Germany and Italy after the sinking of several Brazilian ships.

23rd The Luftwaffe conducted the first major bombing raid on Stalingrad. A rain of incendiary and explosive bombs killed more than 40,000 civilians and reduced most of the city to rubble.

25th A citywide evacuation effort began in Stalingrad. First priority went to specialists and workers whose factories had been destroyed.

28th German submarine U-94 was sunk off Haiti by depth charges from an American PBY Catalina flying boat and ramming by the Canadian corvette Oakville.

29th The German Tiger I tank made its battlefield debut southeast of Leningrad.

September

3rd   Demonstrations and strikes were held throughout Northern Ireland and Eire the day after the execution of Tom Williams. Thomas Joseph Williams, was a volunteer in C Company, 2nd Battalion of the Belfast Brigade in the Irish Republican Army from the Bombay Street area of Belfast, Northern Ireland. He was hanged in the Crumlin Road Gaol for his involvement in the killing of Royal Ulster Constabulary (RUC) police officer named Patrick Murphy during the Northern Campaign.

4th   Service du travail obligatoire: The Vichy French government passed a law requiring all able-bodied men age 18 to 50 and single women 21 to 35 to be subject to do any work the government deemed necessary.

5th   The Soviet 24th and 66th Armies counterattacked the XIV Panzer Corps at Stalingrad, but the offensive was called off after losing 30 of 120 tanks, mostly to the Luftwaffe.

7th   Cuba signed an agreement with the United States allowing a flotilla of a dozen American-manned patrol ships to operate out of Havana under Cuban colours.

8th   The characters of Pogo the Possum and Albert the Alligator made their first appearances in the story "Albert Takes the Cake" by Walt Kelly in Animal Comics issue #1.

10th   The Italian hospital ship Arno was torpedoed and sunk in the Mediterranean by British aircraft.

12th   The Lenin Garrison was destroyed on the 12th September 1942 during a partisan uprising against the Nazis. After the liquidation of the Lenin ghetto in the Pinsk region (now in Belarus) and the murder of its inhabitants on the 14th August 1942, about 30 Jews remained alive in Lenin, as they continued to work directly for the Germans as tailors, shoemakers, builders, and photographers. At this time Lubov Rabinovich was ordered to train a group of Belorussian apprentices to take over his trade within one month.

14th   The New York Yankees clinched the American League pennant with an 8–3 win over the Cleveland Indians.

15th   Near Guadalcanal the Japanese submarine I-19 fired one of the most effective torpedo salvos of the war, mortally damaging the American aircraft carrier USS Wasp and destroyer O'Brien as well as damaging the battleship North Carolina. The destroyer Lansdowne was dispatched to rescue 447 crew of the Hornet and then scuttled the carrier.

September

16th | Laconia incident: A controversial event occurred when a USAAF B-24 Liberator attacked the U-156 while survivors rescued from the September 12 RMS Laconia sinking stood on the foredeck. The U-156 was forced to dive and abandon the survivors. Karl Dönitz shortly thereafter issued the Laconia Order, forbidding any such rescue work in the future.

20th | Nazi authorities killed 116 people in Paris in retaliation for increasing attacks on German officers.

21st | The Boeing B-29 Superfortress had its first test flight.

23rd | Erwin Rommel left North Africa on sick leave, handing over command of the Afrika Korps to Georg Stumme.

24th | The B&O railroad Ambassador train ran into the back of the Cleveland Express near Dickerson, Maryland, killing twelve passengers and two crewmen in the worst B&O accident since 1907.

25th | The aviation-themed action film Desperate Journey starring Errol Flynn and Ronald Reagan was released.

26th | The Manhattan Project was granted approval by the War Production Board to use the highest level of emergency procurement priority. The Manhattan Project was a research and development undertaking during World War II that produced the first nuclear weapons. It was led by the United States with the support of the United Kingdom (which initiated the original Tube Alloys project) and Canada. From 1942 to 1946, the project was under the direction of Major General Leslie Groves of the U.S. Army Corps of Engineers.

27th | German submarine U-165 was depth charged and sunk in the Bay of Biscay by a Vickers Wellington aircraft of No. 311 Squadron RAF.

28th | Joseph Stalin signed an instruction ordering the resumption of the Soviet nuclear research program which had been dormant for a year.

30th | Hitler gave a speech in the Berlin Sportpalast informing his audience that "it will not be the Aryan peoples, but rather Jewry, that will be exterminated."

1st | The first Little Golden Books, a popular series of children's books, were published in the United States. Little Golden Books is a series of children's books, founded in 1942. The eighth book in the series, The Poky Little Puppy, is the top-selling children's book of all time. Many of the Little Golden Books have become bestsellers, including The Poky Little Puppy, Tootle, Scuffy the Tugboat, and The Little Red Hen. Several of the illustrators for the Little Golden Books later became influential within the children's book industry.

3rd | The Hollywood Canteen opened in Hollywood, California. The club was operated and staffed completely by volunteers from the entertainment industry and everything in it was free of charge for Allied servicemen and women in uniform.

4th | Hermann Göring made a speech in the Berlin Sportpalast to mark the end of the harvest season. He announced that Germany's food situation "will continue to get better since we now possess huge stretches of fertile land."

6th | A law was passed in Nazi-occupied Belgium equivalent to the one passed in Vichy France on September 4, obligating able-bodied citizens to do work for the government if ordered to.

8th | A Nazi radio announcement stated that officers and men captured in the Dieppe raid had been manacled in retaliation for the alleged tying of prisoners during the Sark raid. The British War Office replied that German prisoners of war captured at Dieppe had not had their hands tied and if the Germans did not immediately unshackle their prisoners, then German POWs in Canada would be put in chains starting on the 10th October.

9th | Mob boss Roger Touhy and six others escaped from Stateville Correctional Centre in Crest Hill, Illinois. Touhy and his gang would be caught a month later and he would be sentenced to an additional 199 years in prison for the escape.

11th | World heavyweight boxing champion Joe Louis told reporters, "My fighting days are over."

13th | The V2 rocket (number V4) becomes the first man-made object to be launched into space. The V-2 with the technical name Aggregat 4 (A4), was the world's first long-range guided ballistic missile. The missile, powered by a liquid-propellant rocket engine, was developed during the Second World War in Germany as a "vengeance weapon" and assigned to attack Allied cities as retaliation for the Allied bombings against German cities. The V-2 rocket also became the first artificial object to travel into space by crossing the Kármán line with the vertical launch of MW 18014 on the 20th June 1944.

16th | The animated short film The Mouse of Tomorrow, featuring the debut of Mighty Mouse (as "Super Mouse"), was released in the United States.

18th | Adolf Hitler issued the Commando Order stating that all Allied commandos encountered by German forces should be killed immediately without trial, even if they were in proper uniforms or attempted to surrender.

20th | The Art of This Century gallery was opened by Peggy Guggenheim at 30 West 57th Street in Manhattan, New York City on the 20th October 1942. The gallery occupied two commercial spaces on the seventh floor of a building that was part of the midtown arts district including the Museum of Modern Art, the Museum of Non-Objective Painting, Helena Rubinstein's New Art Centre, and numerous commercial galleries.

October

21st   A B-17 carrying Eddie Rickenbacker to conduct an inspection tour of air force facilities in the Pacific and deliver a secret message to Douglas MacArthur went missing en route from Hawaii to Canton Island. The crew had gotten lost and once the plane eventually ran out of fuel and went down, all aboard got into three small life rafts and began a 21-day ordeal drifting in the Pacific.

22nd   The drama film Now, Voyager starring Bette Davis, Paul Henreid and Claude Rains premiered at the Hollywood Theatre in New York City.

23rd   American First Lady Eleanor Roosevelt arrived in London and met with the King and Queen of England at Buckingham Palace.

24th   Operations of the German 6th Army in Stalingrad slowed down considerably due to exhaustion after two weeks of intense fighting as well as the weather growing appreciably colder.

27th   The war film The Navy Comes Through starring Pat O'Brien and George Murphy had its world premiere at Treasure Island Naval Base in San Francisco Bay.

28th   Clark Gable was commissioned as a second lieutenant, earning the right to regrow his famous moustache which he had to shave off when he enlisted.

31st   Two days after signing his first professional contract, 21-year-old Maurice Richard played in his first National Hockey League game for the Montreal Canadians against the Boston Bruins. He recorded an assist during his first NHL shift as the Canadians went on to win 3-2.

November

1st   The Embassy of the Soviet Union posted a bulletin announcing that the Presidium of the Supreme Soviet had formed a committee for the investigation of war crimes committed by the Germans and their associates to the people and property of the USSR.

2nd   The BBC began French-language broadcasts to Canada.

3rd   Erwin Rommel received an order from Adolf Hitler to "stand and die", but disregarded it as plans for a withdrawal were already in place.

5th   Fighting in and around Stalingrad forced the city's power plant to shut down.

6th   The comedy-mystery film Who Done It? starring Abbott and Costello was released.

7th   Joseph Stalin issued an Order of the Day on the 25th anniversary of the October Revolution promising that the enemy "will yet feel the weight of the Red Army's smashing blows."

8th   Hitler made his annual speech in Munich on the 19th anniversary of the Beer Hall Putsch. Hitler claimed that Stalingrad was in German hands with only "a few small pockets" of resistance left.

9th   The American troopship Leedstown, immobilised in the Mediterranean Sea the previous day by an attack from the Luftwaffe, was finished off by a torpedo from German submarine U-331.

November

10th | The comedy film Road to Morocco starring Bing Crosby, Bob Hope and Dorothy Lamour was released.

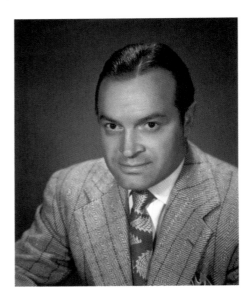 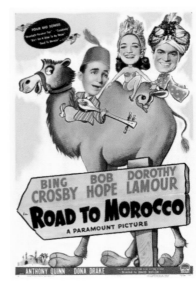 

12th | Eddie Rickenbacker and five others were rescued in the Pacific Ocean after being lost adrift at sea for three weeks. The men had stayed alive on a diet of a few oranges retrieved from their plane when it went down, some fish they'd managed to catch and a seagull that Rickenbacker had grabbed with his bare hands.

13th | Montgomery captured Tobruk, squeezing Rommel between two large advancing Allied forces.

15th | Church bells were rung throughout England in celebration of the Allied victory at El Alamein. It was the first time that church bells had sounded since 1940 when they were silenced during the threat of German invasion.

17th | German submarine U-331 surrendered after being crippled by depth charges from a Lockheed Hudson of No. 500 Squadron RAF north of Algiers. A Fairey Albacore torpedoed and sank the submarine, unaware that the crew had surrendered.

18th | President Roosevelt ordered registration for Selective Service of all youths who had turned 18 since 1st July. This made about 500,000 more Americans eligible for service.

20th | The 1,525-mile Alaska Highway was officially opened. The Alaska Highway was constructed during World War II to connect the contiguous United States to Alaska across Canada. It begins at the junction with several Canadian highways in Dawson Creek, British Columbia, and runs to Delta Junction, Alaska, via Whitehorse, Yukon. When it was completed in 1942, it was about 2,700 kilometres (1,700 mi) long, but in 2012, it was only 2,232 km (1,387 mi). This is due to the continuing reconstruction of the highway, which has rerouted and straightened many sections. The highway opened to the public in 1948. Once legendary for being a rough, challenging drive, the highway is now paved over its entire length. Its component highways are British Columbia Highway 97, Yukon Highway 1 and Alaska Route 2.

21st | The character of Tweety Bird first appeared in the Warner Bros. cartoon A Tale of Two Kitties.

November

22nd | The Robe by Lloyd C. Douglas topped The New York Times Fiction Best Seller list, where it would stay for the rest of the year and much of 1943.

24th | The Japanese destroyer Hayashio was heavily damaged by American planes in the Huon Gulf. The destroyer Shiratsuyu rescued the survivors and then scuttled the ship with a torpedo.

25th | The Germans began airlifting supplies to the 6th Army trapped in Stalingrad. Only 47 Ju 52 transport planes were on hand for the first day, a small fraction of what was needed. Hermann Göring ordered as many Ju 52s as possible to be requisitioned from around occupied Europe to join in the operation.

26th | The romantic drama film Casablanca starring Humphrey Bogart, Ingrid Bergman and Paul Henreid premiered at the Hollywood Theatre in New York City.

27th | Scuttling of the French fleet in Toulon: The French fleet in Toulon was scuttled to keep it out of the hands of German forces. 3 battleships, 7 cruisers, 15 destroyers, 12 submarines and 13 torpedo boats were among the ships scuttled.

 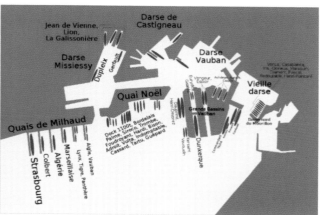

28th | The Army–Navy Game was played in Annapolis, Maryland, with Navy defeating Army 14-0. Only 13,000 spectators saw the game because of a wartime travel restriction that only allowed residents within 10 miles of Annapolis to attend.

29th | The cargo liner Dunedin Star ran aground on the Skeleton Coast of South West Africa. Crew and passengers would spend the next 26 days trekking overland to Windhoek.

30th | The Battle of Tassafaronga was fought off Tassafaronga Point, Guadalcanal, resulting in tactical Japanese victory. Japanese destroyer Takanami was shelled and sunk by the cruiser USS Minneapolis but the American cruiser USS Northampton was torpedoed by Japanese destroyer and sank in the early hours of the 1st December.

December

1st | Fuel rationing began in the United States.

2nd | Manhattan Project: A team of scientists led by Enrico Fermi achieved the first self-sustained nuclear chain reaction at Chicago Pile-1.

December

3rd | Adolf Hitler placed all Axis forces in Tunisia under the newly created Headquarters, 5th Panzer Army and gave the new command to Hans-Jürgen von Arnim.

4th | The swashbuckler film The Black Swan starring Tyrone Power and Maureen O'Hara was released.

5th | Two pilots flew the new American Republic P-47 Thunderbolt fighter plane a record 725 miles per hour.

6th | The horror film Cat People starring Simone Simon, Kent Smith, Tom Conway and Jane Randolph was premiered in New York City.

7th | The Bell P-63 Kingcobra had its first flight. The Bell P-63 Kingcobra is an American fighter aircraft that was developed by Bell Aircraft during World War II. Based on the preceding Bell P-39 Airacobra, the P-63's design incorporated suggestions from P-39 pilots and was superior to its predecessor in virtually all respects. The P-63 was not accepted for combat use by the United States Army Air Forces. However, it was used during World War II by the Soviet Air Force, which had also been the most prolific user of the P-39.

9th | The British corvette Marigold was torpedoed and sunk in the Mediterranean by Italian Savoia-Marchetti SM.79 aircraft with the loss of 40 of her 85 crew.

11th | Italian manned torpedoes and commando frogmen conducted the Raid on Algiers, sinking 2 Allied cargo ships and damaging 3 other vessels although 16 commandos were captured.

12th | Operation Frankton was a commando raid on ships in the German occupied French port of Bordeaux in southwest France during the Second World War. The raid was carried out by a small unit of Royal Marines known as the Royal Marines Boom Patrol Detachment (RMBPD), part of Combined Operations inserted by HMS Tuna captained by Lieutenant-Commander Dick Raikes who, earlier, had been awarded the DSO for operations while in command of the submarine HMS Seawolf (47S). (The RMBPD would later form the Special Boat Service). The plan was for six kayaks (called "canoes" by the British) to be taken to the area of the Gironde estuary by submarine. Twelve men would then paddle by night to Bordeaux. On arrival they would attack the docked cargo ships with limpet mines and then escape overland to Spain.

December

13th	The Washington Redskins defeated the Chicago Bears 14–6 in the NFL Championship Game played at Griffith Stadium in Washington, D.C.
15th	German submarine U-626 was depth charged and sunk in the Atlantic Ocean by the U.S. Coast Guard cutter Ingham.
17th	The Volga River finally froze over, allowing Soviet forces in Stalingrad to be resupplied.
18th	Benito Mussolini sent Galeazzo Ciano to meet with Hitler at the Wolf's Lair. Ciano carried Mussolini's message urging Hitler to seek a separate peace with the Soviets, but Hitler strongly rejected the idea.
24th	Soviet tanks broke through German defences at Tatsinskaya Airfield in Rostov Oblast, an important airfield flying supplies to Stalingrad. 124 Ju 52 transport planes were able to evacuate, but 46 other aircraft were damaged, destroyed or left behind.
25th	Pope Pius XII delivered the Christmas address over Vatican Radio denouncing the extermination of people based on race, though it was carefully worded in general terms rather than specifically condemning the Nazis.
27th	The fifth National Football League All-Star Game was held at Shibe Park in Philadelphia. An all-star team defeated the Washington Redskins 17–14.
28th	Hitler issued Directive No. 47, concerning command and defence measures in the southeast. The directive referred to the possibility of attacks in the region of Crete and the Balkans.
30th	Frank Sinatra performed his first solo concert at the Paramount Theatre in New York City. Sinatra later recalled being "scared stiff" when the audience of 5,000 bobby soxers shrieked and screamed continuously for America's new teen idol.
31st	The Battle of the Barents Sea was fought between the Kriegsmarine and British ships escorting convoy JW 51B to Kola Inlet. The British destroyer Achates was sunk while the Germans lost the destroyer Z16 Friedrich Eckoldt. All 14 merchant ships reached their destination so the battle was a strategic British victory.
	Hitler issued an Order of the Day to the German armed forces declaring, "The year 1943 will perhaps be hard but certainly not harder than the one just behind us."

PEOPLE IN POWER

John Curtin
1941-1945
Australia
Prime Minister

Philippe Pétain
1940-1944
France
Président

Getúlio Vargas
1930-1945
Brazil
President

William Mackenzie
1935-1948
Canada
Prime Minister

Lin Sen
1931-1943
China
Government of China

Adolf Hitler
1934-1945
Germany
Führer of Germany

Marquess of Linlithgow
1936-1943
India
Viceroy of India

Benito Mussolini
1922-1943
Italy
President

Hirohito
1926-1989
Japan
Emperor

Manuel Ávila Camacho
1940-1946
Mexico
President

Joseph Stalin
1922-1952
Russia
Premier

Jan Smuts
1939-1948
South Africa
Prime Minister

Franklin D. Roosevelt
1933-1945
United States
President

Hubert Pierlot
1939-1945
Belgium
Prime Minister

Peter Fraser
1939-1949
New Zealand
Prime Minister

Sir Winston Churchill
1940-1945
United Kingdom
Prime Minister

Per Albin Hansson
1936-1946
Sweden
Prime Minister

Christian X
1912-1947
Denmark
King

Francisco Franco
1936-1975
Spain
President

Miklós Horthy
1920-1944
Hungary
Kingdom of Hungary

The Year You Were Born 1942
Book by Sapphire Publishing

Printed in Great Britain
by Amazon